Access your online resources

Helping Children with Loss is accompanied by a number of printable online materials, designed to ensure this resource best supports your professional needs

Activate your online resources:

Go to www.routledge.com/cw/speechmark and click on the cover of this book
Click the 'Sign in or Request Access' button and follow the instructions in order to access the resources

Helping Children with Loss

Now in a fully updated second edition, this professional guidebook has been created to help adults provide emotional support for children who have experienced the loss of somebody they know, or something they loved.

Written in an accessible style and with a sensitive tone, *Helping Children with Loss* provides adults with a rich vocabulary for mental states and painful emotions, paving the way for meaningful and healing conversations with children who are struggling with difficult feelings. Practical activities provide opportunities for conversation and will empower the child to find creative and imaginative ways of expressing themselves when words fail.

Key features of this resource include:

- Targeted advice for children who defend against feeling their painful feelings by dissociating from grief
- Tools and strategies for helping children cope with loss, including engaging activities to help children explore their feelings in a non-threatening way
- Photocopiable and downloadable resources to help facilitate support

Written by a leading child psychotherapist with over thirty years' experience, this book will support children to develop emotional literacy and connect with unresolved feelings affecting their behaviour. It is an essential resource for anybody supporting children aged 4–12 who have experienced loss.

Margot Sunderland is Director of Education and Training at The Centre for Child Mental Health London, Co-Director of Trauma Informed Schools UK, Honorary Visiting Fellow at London Metropolitan University, Senior Associate Member of the Royal College of Medicine, and Child Psychotherapist with over thirty years' experience of working with children, teenagers (many in residential care homes) and families. She is also a qualified secondary school teacher.

Margot is author of over twenty books in the field of child mental health, which collectively have been translated into eighteen languages and published in twenty-four countries. Her internationally acclaimed book, *The Science of Parenting* won a first prize in the British Medical Association Medical Book awards and has been voted as one of the best brain books of our time by The Dana Foundation. Dr Sunderland has been studying the neuroscience of adult-child relationships for seventeen years. Dr Sunderland is also founding Director of The Institute for Arts in Therapy and Education, a Higher Education College and Academic Partner of University of East London. The College runs master's degrees/diplomas in Child Psychotherapy, Child Counselling, Parent-Child Therapy and Therapeutic Play.

Nicky Armstrong holds an MA from the Slade School of Fine Art and a BA Hons in Theatre Design from the University of Central England. She has illustrated over thirty-four books in the mental health field, which have been translated into five languages/countries. She works full time as an illustrator and fine artist. She has achieved major commissions nationally and internationally in mural work and fine art.

Helping Children with Feelings

Margot Sunderland's bestselling series of therapeutic stories for children, each accompanied by a professional guidebook, is designed to help children aged 4–12 connect with unresolved feelings affecting their behaviour.

Using Story Telling as a Therapeutic Tool with Children

Helping Children with Loss: A Guidebook (2e)
The Day the Sea Went Out and Never Came Back: A Story for Children Who Have Lost Someone They Love (2e)

Helping Children Pursue Their Hopes and Dreams: A Guidebook
A Pea Called Mildred: A Story to Help Children Pursue Their Hopes and Dreams

Helping Children who Bottle Up Their Feelings: A Guidebook
A Nifflenoo Called Nevermind: A Story for Children who Bottle Up Their Feelings

Helping Children who have Hardened Their Hearts or Become Bullies: A Guidebook
A Wibble Called Bipley: A Story for Children who have Hardened Their Hearts or Become Bullies

Helping Children who are Anxious or Obsessional: A Guidebook
Willy and the Wobbly House: A Story for Children who are Anxious and Obsessional

Helping Children Who Yearn for Someone They Love: A Guidebook
The Frog Who Longed for the Moon to Smile: A Story for Children who Yearn for Someone They Love

Helping Children Locked in Rage or Hate: A Guidebook
How Hattie Hated Kindness: A Story for Children Locked in Rage or Hate

Helping Children with Fear: A Guidebook
Teenie Weenie in a Too Big World: A Story for Fearful Children

Helping Children with Low Self-Esteem: A Guidebook
Ruby and the Rubbish Bin: A Story for Children with Low Self-Esteem

Helping Children of Troubled Parents: A Guidebook
Monica Plum's Horrid Problem: A Story for Children of Troubled Parents

Helping Children with Loss

A Guidebook

Second Edition

MARGOT SUNDERLAND
ILLUSTRATED BY NICKY ARMSTRONG

Cover image: Nicky Armstrong.

Second edition published 2022
by Routledge
4 Park Square, Milton Park, Abingdon, Oxon, OX14 4RN

and by Routledge
605 Third Avenue, New York, NY 10158

Routledge is an imprint of the Taylor & Francis Group, an informa business

© 2022 Margot Sunderland and Nicky Armstrong

The right of Margot Sunderland to be identified as author of this work and Nicky Armstrong to be identified as illustrator of this work has been asserted in accordance with sections 77 and 78 of the Copyright, Designs and Patents Act 1988.

All rights reserved. The purchase of this copyright material confers the right on the purchasing institution to photocopy or download pages which bear the companion website icon and a copyright line at the bottom of the page. No other parts of this book may be reprinted or reproduced or utilised in any form or by any electronic, mechanical, or other means, now known or hereafter invented, including photocopying and recording, or in any information storage or retrieval system, without permission in writing from the publishers.

Trademark notice: Product or corporate names may be trademarks or registered trademarks, and are used only for identification and explanation without intent to infringe.

First edition published by Speechmark 2003

British Library Cataloguing-in-Publication Data
A catalogue record for this book is available from the British Library

Library of Congress Cataloging-in-Publication Data
Names: Sunderland, Margot, author. | Armstrong, Nicky, illustrator.
Title: Helping children with loss : a guidebook / Margot Sunderland ; illustrated by Nicky Armstrong.
Description: Second Edition. | New York : Routledge, 2022. | Series: Helping children with feelings | Includes bibliographical references and index.
Identifiers: LCCN 2021040050 (print) | LCCN 2021040051 (ebook) | ISBN 9781032101910 (Paperback) | ISBN 9781003214113 (eBook)
Subjects: LCSH: Loss (Psychology) in children.
Classification: LCC BF723.L68 S59 2022 (print) | LCC BF723.L68 (ebook) | DDC 155.4/124—dc23/eng/20211117
LC record available at https://lccn.loc.gov/2021040050
LC ebook record available at https://lccn.loc.gov/2021040051

ISBN: 978-1-032-10191-0 (pbk)
ISBN: 978-1-003-21411-3 (ebk)

DOI: 10.4324/9781003214113

Typeset in DIN Pro
by Apex CoVantage, LLC

Access the companion website: www.routledge.com/cw/speechmark

Contents

Introduction 1
1 Helping grieving children with their painful feelings 3
2 Helping grieving children who defend against feeling their painful feelings 25
3 Practical ways of enabling children to speak about and work through feelings of loss 43
Bibliography 81
Index 90

Note on the text

For the sake of clarity alone, throughout the text the child has been referred to as 'he' and the parent as 'she'. Unless otherwise stated, for clarity alone, where 'mummy,' 'mother' or 'mother figure' is used, this refers to either parent or other primary caretaker.

Confidentiality

Where appropriate, full permission has been granted by adults, or children and their parents, to use therapeutic case material. Other illustrations comprise synthesised and disguised examples to ensure anonymity.

Introduction

> And when you left
> I hung my lifeless life,
> Like long unchosen garment,
> In the dark belly of some forgotten wardrobe,
> *and will you know?*
>
> *Margot Sunderland*

This book is all about helping children with the pain of loss. Children need this help just as much as adults, because often they don't know how to grieve – they need an adult in their life who is emotionally literate and can help them put their sorrow into words. A vast body of research shows that, for children, talking about traumatic loss to an adult trained to listen, trained to help them think about their mental states instead of just experiencing their mental states, is extremely protective against both long-term physical and mental ill-health (e.g. Fonagy and Bateman, 2006; Burklund et al., 2014).

If we don't provide emotional support for grieving children, sadly many will go on to develop long-term mental and physical health problems. For example, one longitudinal study found that bottling up feelings increases the risk of cancer by 70 per cent (Chapman et al., 2013). Many other studies show a direct link between the inability to put painful feelings into words and somatisation, eating disorders, depression and anxiety (e.g. Shipko, 1982; Honkalampi, 2000; Karukivi, 2010; Casagrande et al., 2019; Lyvers et al., 2019; Fang et al., 2020). Research shows that children who feel miserable but cannot say why are far more likely to become depressed than children who are able to accurately label their painful feelings (Starr et al., 2020).

This book is designed to support you with a rich vocabulary for mental states and painful emotions, so that you can have the most meaningful and healing conversations when helping children with loss. For children, however, words alone may fail to do justice to their feelings. Children need images, stories and play to help them speak well. This book also supports you with many images to help children talk about their feelings.

Painful feelings of loss that are not symbolised into words or images (e.g. through drawings, art, sand play) remain at sensation level – the 'unthought known' – *'I know it, but I have not yet had a thought about it'* (Bollas, 1987). As put by Fang et al. (2020), *'Unprocessed distressing feelings bring disturbances in both physical and psychological health.'*

DOI: 10.4324/9781003214113-1

Introduction

Research shows that emotional awareness and the ability to put words to painful feelings, such as those of traumatic loss, prevents depression and anxiety and symptoms of internalised distress, such as self-harm or rumination, and calms both body and mind (Rieffe and De Rooij, 2012; Burklund et al., 2014). As beautifully put by Angus and Greenberg (2011), *'Regulation of underregulated emotion occurs through the ability to symbolise emotions so that the person is having the emotion rather than to emotion having the person.'*

1. Helping grieving children with their painful feelings

That moment of loss when someone the child has loved deeply leaves or dies can herald a complex mix of agonising feelings: despair, futility, anger, fear, shock, emptiness, to name a few. The strength of the feelings and the pain of the grief can, at times, feel too much to endure. Oh, to feel just the comparative sweetness of sadness rather than this acute ache, this searing, screaming pain. Because of the intensity of grief, children and adults can at times feel almost crazy and/or that they cannot go on.

So, when working with children who are suffering the pain of loss, we need to be very aware of the whole range of feelings and mental states they may be experiencing. This knowledge will inform our empathic responses, which are key to healing (Gottman et al., 1996). We will fail grieving children if we just talk to them about being sad. With traumatic loss, so many more feelings are involved, all needing to be spoken about and addressed.

This chapter is designed to support you in your work, with an exploration of some of the commonest emotional responses to loss in order to inform your empathic statements.

Helping grieving children with shock

'The awful thing had happened, and no-one had stopped it.' These were the words of Gemma, aged eight, talking about the death of her mother.

It is easy to begin to think that your life will carry on down the same path, with roughly the same people. Then one day something happens that changes everything. This happens with loss: loss of a loved one; loss of a school friend; loss of your home or school (when children experience multiple moves). And so often these losses lead to other losses: loss of so much that is safe and known in your life; loss of trust; loss of self-esteem. Things are literally never the same again. When a child suffers a traumatic loss, it is in effect the ending of his life as he has known it.

Terrible shocks are something most of us have to manage at some time in our life. Yet the parenting and education we receive provide us with few, if any, resources to know how to cope well with shocks. Without help to feel, think about and work through

DOI: 10.4324/9781003214113-2

shock states, negative reverberations can cause long-term psychological problems. Also, when it is denied, shock can get locked in the body, resulting in all manner of illnesses and physical symptoms. As Bessel van der Kolk (2015), a famous researcher in traumatic stress states, writes, *'The body keeps the score.'* Shock states can also badly affect the ability to concentrate at school, to make good decisions, and to function well on all levels. In traumatic stress we become frightened unthinking animals. Shock is so often experienced as a body blow. The child may literally feel 'shattered' by it.

The child's bodily response to the shock may include loss of appetite, bed-wetting, nightmares, and wanting to shake and scream.

How you can help

1) **Offer children repeated times with an emotionally available adult who will be alongside them with their outpouring of grief in a totally non-judgemental way**. Children lucky enough to have such a trusted and emotionally available adult after traumatic loss can be supported to release the shock trapped in their body.

2) **Give psychoeducation**. Children who understand can benefit from knowing that it is emotionally and physically healthy to let shock out of your body. So, give the child permission to let the shock out by crying and shaking. Tell them about animals. When, for example, a wildebeest is carried in the mouth of a lion but gets away, it will shake afterwards to release the fear and shock from its body. Humans often fight against this, which is not good for their physical or mental health. As Maudsley (founder of the London hospital of that name) said many years ago: *'The sorrow that hath no vent in tears makes other organs weep'* (cited in McDougall, 1989). It may help to talk to children, when appropriate, about the cost to emotional health of bottling up feelings of shock, and to praise them hugely for their courage in expressing it.

3) **Help children with words to use**. Use the word 'shock.' Often children are in shock and don't realise they are. It really helps them to know about shock, as it makes sense of what they are experiencing. They then need to be able to talk about the feeling of shock. In this endeavour, it is often useful to use the exercise in Chapter 3 called Shock states. This exercise aims to help children to address their shock states, and to find words for their feelings, so that their pain can begin to be modified. For some children, the exercise may be the first time they have acknowledged to themselves the power of the shock, and awareness is a vital stage in the healing process.

4) **Encourage children to find their power again**. Shock often leaves children feeling helpless and impotent, so encourage them to take their power back by finding an angry response to what happened. Drums are ideal for this, as is writing angry words

on paper. So rather than the retreating and withdrawing of powerlessness and hopelessness, you are encouraging the child to feel the energy of aggressing on the world. Martha, aged 11, for example, found it particularly healing to draw 'Cancer, I hate you. How dare you take my mum.'

5) **Offer quotes like the following, which may help**.

> *You've survived 100 per cent of your worst days.* (unknown)
>
> *At any given moment, you have the power to say: this is not how the story is going to end.* (Christine Mason Miller)
>
> *One bad chapter does not mean your story is over.* (unknown)

6) **Make empathic statements about shock states**. Examples include:
   - Everything got smashed up that day.
   - It was like your world ended that day.
   - Because you are in shock, you need to be very kind and gentle to yourself, and other people need to be kind and gentle to you too.
   - You may feel disorientated, because you are. You are now in a different world than before – a world before the bad thing happened – so it's a very disorientating world.

- ◐ When you lose someone you have deeply loved and they are not ever going to come back, it's always a terrible shock and your life is changed for ever. It is changed but not destroyed, although at first it may feel as though it is destroyed.
- ◐ After a big shock, you can feel very different inside.
- ◐ After a big shock, your whole body is in a state of alarm.

7) **Consider PTSD (post-traumatic stress disorder)**. If a long time has passed since the child experienced the event and yet he is still suffering from persistent hyperarousal, hypervigilance, flashbacks, generalised anxiety, startle reactions, problems sleeping, etc.; then he is probably suffering from PTSD. In PTSD, core arousal and stress response systems in the brain can be affected, making the body unable to regulate its internal systems properly; this can result in problems with sleeping, eating and digestion, and the immune system doesn't work well, which can cause physical ailments. If the child has any of the above-mentioned symptoms, refer him to a PTSD specialist (unless you are one yourself, of course). EMDR (eye movement desensitising reprocessing) or CBT (cognitive behaviour therapy) are particularly successful in treating PTSD (Khan et al., 2018).

Helping grieving children cope with the awful pain

What happens to the brain chemistry of children who love someone deeply?

When an attachment bond between two people is deeply loving, then at times of intimacy – shared delightful play states, when comforting distress, or in moments of real emotional connection – the brain's emotion chemicals and the body's hormones, released in both people, feel exquisite. When flowing strongly, it is these chemicals and hormones that make a child feel warm and tender, deeply content, and that all is well in his world. This is far more than just a state of calm that you might get from looking at the sea, for example. It is a far richer response, and results in feeling expansive, potent and very loved.

These powerful natural chemicals, released in interactions with a loved person, are oxytocin and opioids. As Panksepp, founder of affective neuroscience, and with over 40 years in a laboratory studying emotional systems in the brain, says, *'Brain oxytocin and opioids systems appear to be the key participants in these subtle feelings that we humans call acceptance, nurturance and love and warmth.'* Panksepp states that optimally activated opioids and oxytocin in the brain's CARE system are *'nature's gifts to us'* (Panksepp and Biven, 2012).

The language of loss is the language of pain.

Panksepp also says,

> *When this feeling of normalcy is suddenly disrupted by the undesired loss . . . or the unexpected death of a loved one, we find ourselves plunged into one of the deepest and most troubling emotional pains of which we, as social creatures are capable. The psychic pain informs us of the importance of those we have lost.*
>
> (Panksepp, 1998)

When a child loses someone he loved deeply, the wonderful hormones and brain chemicals described above are no longer dominant in his brain, and other painful neurochemical systems take over. This results in acute psychological pain. Hence the child who loved someone deeply will suffer terribly if that person dies or leaves. There is no getting away from this – it is how the human brain and body are genetically programmed.

The natural brain opioids released when a child deeply loves a parent are addictive. As Panksepp says, '*Social bonds are to some extent mediated by opioid-based, naturally occurring addictive processes within the brain*' (Panksepp and Biven, 1998). Losing a loved one is, therefore, as painful and as powerful as coming off heroin. (Heroin activates the opioid system in our brains or, looked at vice versa, opioids mimic the action of heroin in our brains.) We are all familiar with films of people coming off such drugs – the agony, the torment. The same emotions are experienced by the child who has lost a loved one.

For the grieving child, the intensity of the pain can feel unbearable. Scientists have found that loss of a loved one triggers the same pain centres in the brain as when we are in physical pain (Eisenberger, 2012). The neurochemicals of painful loss block all pleasure and wellbeing chemicals such as opioids and dopamine; hence, in grief, some children feel no pleasure in anything. '*Psychological pain and loneliness are promoted by high levels of stress-promoting corticotropin-releasing factor (CRF) and a dearth of soothing opioids. When opioids are low, and CRF is running high, people and animals feel lonely, distressed, and miserable*' (Panksepp and Biven, 2012).

How the pain of loss can hit children in fits and starts

Sometimes he is seemingly playing happily, and adults worry that he is denying his grief. Then suddenly he is overwhelmed by grief: '*I just want my mummy, I want my mummy, I want my mummy . . .*' he howls and howls, as if forever. Adults in his life may worry that they themselves will not be able to stand the agony of his calling, it is so raw and terrible. All too often, it screams an intensity that makes them remember things in their own lives they have been trying to forget.

Loss of a deeply loved person is one of the most intensely painful experiences we can suffer. It can bring torment and anguish. It can feel as if nothing but the return of the lost person could bring comfort. And yet many people think that children do not feel grief as intensely as adults. This is not the case, as we know from the neurobiology of grief. In fact, because children fall deeply in love with their parents, they are just as vulnerable as adults to the agony of lost love.

Children often give the impression that after the loss of a loved one, life resumes as normal. This is partly because of their limited language skills, and partly because young children are genetically programmed with powerful motoric impulses that cannot yet be inhibited. So, after their loss, young children will still run and leap and climb and play ball. To an adult who associates grief with sitting very still and being very introverted and withdrawn, this high level of motoric activity seems to indicate a lack of grief. So, when the grieving child is swinging on the high bar and playing tag with his friends, parents may think, *'He seems to be adjusting well.'* Then, like a plane flying into sudden turbulence, the child moves into bursts of heartbreaking crying.

For children, the pain of loss can touch everything. Even the very sense of who they are can be deeply affected. The loss changes not only how they view the world, but how they view themselves. C.S. Lewis, for example, found one of the hardest things about his wife's death was her physical absence in terms of *his own* body and self. He said, *'There is one place where her absence comes locally home to me, and it is a place I can't avoid. I mean my own body . . . Now it's like an empty house'* (Lewis, 1966, p.12).

James, aged three
When he was three, James lost his beloved daddy to lung cancer. Any outsider could see how desperately in love James had been with his adorable daddy. When James was upset, his daddy would stroke his back and say, *'I know, I know.'* After his father's death, whenever James was upset, he would say to himself out loud, *'I know, I know.'* Because James continued to run around, ride his bike with enormous vigour and play rough-and-tumble with his friends, observers may have thought that James had got over the loss of his daddy. But as James developed more language skills, he started to refer increasingly to his daddy. Suddenly, in the middle of a conversation about something entirely different, or in the middle of a car ride or building a sandcastle, he would speak about his daddy. Seemingly out of nowhere he would say, *'My daddy can't see my legs*

anymore' or '*My daddy didn't want to go*' or '*Cigarettes took my daddy. They shouldn't have.*' One day, while eating an ice cream on the beach, he expressed his anger at his mother: '*You should have chosen another one, you should have chosen another one*' (meaning you should have chosen a different man to be your husband, one who didn't smoke).

Terry, aged seven

Terry, whose mother had died the previous year, came home from school one day and told his dad that he had had a great day. When asked why, Terry said: '*One of my friends, Sabina, told me her uncle, whom she loved like a dad, has died.*' Terry told his dad that at last didn't feel odd, different, and so alone in his grief. Something huge and terrible had happened to him, and yet no one had talked about it and no other child seemed to understand. Now at last Sabina did.

How you can help

1) **Respect their timing about when they want to talk about it**. Often, out of the blue, the young child drops a most painful statement about his grief, his longing and his yearning into the conversation. The caring adult then comes in with empathy, only to find that the child has gone off again into some new motoric activity, to revisit his grief in his own time and at his own pace. It's like a bird who swoops, picks up the worm and then is off again. His timing needs to be respected. When an adult can truly feel into the child's pain, without trying to fix him, but listens and understands, 'the bird' will return many times. Do not be fooled into thinking that a child seems unaffected by the loss. Follow his rhythm. Do not try to force him to stay with his talk about his grief longer than he wants to. Let the bird fly off.

2) **Don't try to make the child feel better in the sense of trying to bring about a quick recovery from his grief**. When you are grieving, that can just make you feel worse and that it is unsafe to open up. Rather, just listen and be with him in his grieving process.

3) **Don't stay silent in the face of his crying or talking about his pain**. To the child, this can feel like being abandoned at his most vulnerable. Sometimes the best response is just to say something softly, such as, '*I am so, so sorry that happened to you*' or '*So painful... So hard.*' Short phrases like these in a gentle, caring, soothing voice let children know that you are there for them and they are no longer alone with their grief.

4) **Avoid reassurances**. It is so tempting not to respond to a child's pain in the way described above, because his pain can cause you pain. The temptation is to go into reassurances; for example, '*But I think you are lovely!*' or '*It's not that bad, you have xxx still in your life.*' Reassurances never reassure. Reassurances mean you can't bear the pain in the room. Stay with the pain. Remember your attention, your active listening;

you're enabling the child to feel met in his pain. To feel truly understood (maybe for the first time by anyone) brings a child a sense of being deeply valued, that he matters, that what he is feeling matters. This is the hope and the healing. Also, remember, *'Previously unmanageable feelings become more manageable, they become less terrifying than before, because another person has actually felt them and has been able to tolerate the experience of those feelings'* (Casement, 2013).

5) **If there wasn't a goodbye, suggest the child might like to write a note or letter**. This is because loss is essentially lost connection, and so a letter can feel like a way of connecting. Writing a note or message on a pebble and putting it into the sea can feel particularly healing.

6) **Offer comfort**. Through the neuroscience of comforting, we know that painful feelings can be partially relieved because accepting the comforting of the other, releases opioids and oxytocin within our brains These are wellbeing, anti-anxiety neurochemicals.

7) **Ensure the child has alternative modes of expressing his grief, rather than everyday words**. A child who is in pain with loss but unable to find the words to express his feelings will tend to show the grief through his behaviour. In particular, such feelings may be seen in behaviours that challenge, learning difficulties, sleeping or eating problems; nightmares; sudden angry or raging behaviour; or just a general withdrawing and cutting-off. So, ensure he has, for example, art materials, sandplay and/or clay to symbolise his pain. Once he has expressed his pain in this way, he will no longer need to express it through behaviour.

8) **Communicate these key messages for the child in pain** (in age-appropriate language).
   - It is brave to dare to love because it hurts so much to lose that love. But you dared to love, and it brought beautiful things to your world that now remain as memories . . .
   - Lovely memories of the person who is gone or dead are like treasure in your mind that no one can take away.
   - The more we have loved, the more we will hurt if we lose the person we love. So, if you are really hurting now, it means you had the courage to really love someone.
   - Missing can hurt a lot, just like a broken limb or a cut knee. You just want the pain to go away. Physical pain needs medicine. But for emotional pain, the best medicine is telling someone you really like and trust all about how much you hurt and, if you are brave enough, to let yourself cry in front of that person.
   - The pain of losing someone you love is normal and is intense unless you are defending against it. Unless dying young, no-one can escape the pain of loss at some time in their life.

🐚 Thousands of years ago, a very wise playwright said, *'We inherit grief just by virtue of being born human'* (Euripides, in *Electra*, around 413 BC). He was right: grief is a fact of life; it cannot be avoided. Some children never know the pain of loss until they are grown-ups. It is difficult for a child to know it. Sometimes a child is wiser about the pain of loss than some adults who have not yet suffered it or who have not dared to feel the pain of it. Sometimes it is difficult for other adults and other children to really understand properly about a child's pain. But some people really do understand. And you will know when you have found a person who really can understand.

Helping grieving children with their feelings of emptiness: when the world turns cold and bleak

No more Mummy

> Because she's gone,
> There's just the dizzy and the strange
> Of too much scatter in the swirl;
> So I'm this skull of flung and lost
> That cannot move the vastness from its eyes,
> These withered sacks for eyes which have no sight of her
> In this too lonely steep of night.
>
> Because she's gone,
> I cannot let her know
> About the jagged bits of fall and creep
> That's clinging to the chill of air,
> About these ceaseless floats of speck
> That push themselves into my face,
> About there is no you.
> And there will be no days, no days
> And there will be no days.
>
> *Margot Sunderland*

If you are a child who has lost someone you loved deeply, the world can have a terrible bleakness and a terrible rawness. A child can feel that the person who left or died took too much away – sometimes even took away a vital part of who he is, for example his hope, his sense of self, his reason for living, his happiness. It's like living in a world that has lost its colour and beauty.

This feeling often affects the child's perception of everything. In other words, because his inner world is so bleak, he can begin to see his outer world as bleak too.
He no longer hears the birds singing. He no longer feels the warmth of the sun on his skin. He no longer relishes the taste of his favourite ice cream at the beach. All is experienced as cold and bleak: people as well as things. If a child is not given the opportunity to speak about the bleakness and emptiness and grieve his loss in the presence of an emotionally available adult, some will withdraw, cutting themselves off from warm contact of friends or other loved ones who were once vital sources of emotional nourishment.

When experiencing traumatic loss, some children feel acutely lonely, particularly if there is no alternative attachment figure in their life to whom they can spontaneously turn for comfort. That heartache can feel ever present and can be particularly strong when the child is in places that he associates with his lost person. Such places are literally and symbolically emptied of all value and goodness.

Ajah, aged ten
Ajah had lost his mother. He no longer wanted to play with his friends. His schoolwork went downhill and day after day he was reported by school staff as just staring out of the

window in his lessons. In this place of isolation, Ajah was putting himself further and further away from the comfort and goodness in his world.

How you can help

1) **Children who have no loving, comforting adult in their life after their loss should be prioritised for school counselling or therapy.** The pain of losing a loved one is all the more agonising if the child has no other loved parent figure to whom he can turn for comfort. Then his world is truly a bleak wilderness.
2) **Help the child to symbolise their bleakness through art media.** When children feel as if the loss has plunged them into a world bereft of warmth, love and kindness, it's vital to give them art media to express their feelings. Then they can step back from the bleakness rather than become the bleakness. You can, for example, ask children to draw their life before the loss as a place and their life now as a place, so you can really understand their perception.

Examples of children whose grief was imbued with feelings of emptiness and who found solace talking about their feelings in story writing, art or sandplay with an emotionally available adult

Alvina, aged 12
Her mother died when she was six. She told this story when she was ten.

'The sun falls out of the sky. Sometimes I feel like I fall out of the sky too. Everything lovely has fallen out of everything and got lost at the bottom of the world. I sometimes feel as if I live at the bottom of the world now.'

Amani, aged 11
Amani's single mother left her, and Amani was put into care. Amani said: *'The world's too cold. It could smash me up with its coldness.'*

Stella, aged 12
Stella lost her mother when she was eight. (Her father had left a long time ago.) This is her picture of vases with no flowers, houses with no windows, and parents with no smiles. She says there is a biting wind and people walk along with hate in their eyes.

Emma, aged 13

Here is a reconstruction of Emma's sandplay picture called 'No Man's Land.' When Emma was seven, her father, whom she loved dearly, left to live abroad with another woman.

Helping grieving children cope with fear

For some children, their traumatic loss is experienced as a catastrophe. They may then develop catastrophic fantasies that they will suffer further losses. So, for example, when a child loses one parent, he can be terrified of losing the other. There can be a feeling of *'What else is going to crash-land in my life?'*

After the death of a parent, separation anxiety from the other parent is very common. *'Something might happen to Mummy while I'm at school, so I hate school. I don't want to go to school any more.'* This is often not spoken as such until someone takes the time to sit down with the child and ask him about his fears why it is so difficult to leave Mummy at the school gate. In examples such as this, school phobias are not in fact phobias about school, but rather a terror of separation from the remaining parent. Separation anxiety can lead to morbid preoccupations that the remaining parent will die in a car crash or be kidnapped, murdered, etc. This fear of no reunion is fuelled by the fact that when the loved one died, there *was* no reunion.

Other children may develop fears of going mad, or fears of the strength of their wish to be dead – that they might actually act on it – or fear of their heart is actually breaking. This is not as irrational as it may sound. A clear link has been found between adults who suffer from depression or feel hopeless and heart attacks (Anda et al., 1993).

Additionally, a professor at the National Heart, Lung and Blood Institute in the USA said, *'Thirty years of epidemiological data indicate that depression does predict the development of heart disease'* (Stewart, 2017). Research shows that compared with people without depression, adults with a depressive disorder or symptoms have a 64 per cent greater risk of developing coronary artery disease (Patel et al, 2018).

Nikkita, aged eight
When Nikkita was five, her daddy died. After that, she was beside herself whenever her mother went out of the house without her. She was sure that this was the last time she would see her mummy. Nikkita would move all her books in front of the door in an attempt to barricade her mother in the house. Nikkita was also terrified if Mummy got a common cold (imagined in Nikkita's head as the start of a downward slope which would end with her mummy dying).

Alesha, aged eleven

Alesha's father had died when she was six, and she was now terrified of her mother dying, and so screamed and clung to her mother when she was dropped at school.

How you can help

1) **Tell children how their past experience can colour their perception of the present.** Children whose loss has triggered repeated fear states can be helped enormously by information about how the mind works and how the FEAR circuit in the lower brain (subcortex) can become trigger-happy and react to the present and the future as if there were about to be a repeat of the past. The problem is, the higher brain will not say, *'Hey, you are remembering something.'* Instead, the lower-brain alarm systems (e.g. the amygdala) will make you believe it is about the here and now. With this knowledge about the brain, the child is usually more able to mentalise (reflect on his mental states) and test reality, and to say to himself, *'Hang on, you are muddling up what happened to you when Mum died with terrifying fears about the future.'*

2) Some children are reassured by such phrases as, 'There are few jokers in the pack' and '90 percent of what we worry about never happens' (Jeffers, 2012). It is called reassurance reality testing. But for other children it would be inappropriate and like water off a duck's back as they need far more in-depth help.

3) If you feel the child has become stuck in the fear and shock of the loss and over time is just not getting better, in fact, symptoms are getting worse; then we suggest you look for a PTSD specialist. Research shows that a trauma specialist trained in EMDR

(eye movement desensitisation and reprocessing) is more effective than trauma-focused CBT (de Roos et al., 2011)

4) Watch out for symptoms that the child might be suffering from PTSD (post-traumatic stress) and so may need a referral to a PTSD specialist. Here are some of the key symptoms (adapted from American Psychiatric Association DSM-5 2013):

Marked alterations in arousal and reactivity.
Irritable behaviour and angry outbursts (with little or no provocation), typically expressed as verbal or physical aggression toward people or objects.
Reckless or self-destructive behaviour.
Hypervigilance.
Exaggerated startle response.
Problems with concentration.
Sleep disturbance (e.g. difficulty falling or staying asleep or restless sleep).

Helping grieving children who are yearning, longing or searching

> *Some bereaved people are conscious of their urge to search, others are not ... Whatever attitude a bereaved person takes towards the urge ... he none the less finds himself impelled to search and, if possible, to recover the person who has gone.*
>
> (Bowlby, 1978)

The urge to search for a lost loved one is genetically ingrained in us. Animals who lose a parent also begin searching. In studies of infant monkeys separated from their mothers, they initially search frantically and make distress calls, but eventually become passive and sink into a hopeless resigned state.

A child who has lost a loved one may move into all kinds of symbolic and displaced searching activities. The searching for the lost loved one can so easily become transferred to material objects. With younger children who have lost a loved one, the loss of their doll or a toy car can seem like a total tragedy, and may elicit all manner of manic searching activities, with desperate bouts of crying. The child may say or call the lost person's name, or search for the lost person, even if he knows on some level that it is irrational.

Yearning for the lost person can be transferred unconsciously on to something or someone else, which then may become an obsession. When a child's strength of feeling and the often relentlessness of yearning is too unbearable, it can be displaced (totally out of conscious awareness) on to yearning for something else. A common displaced yearning is wanting new things all the time. As soon as one thing is bought, the next thing in the shop window is yearned for. Or the child may yearn for comfort substitutes, for example chocolate or a drink – *'I'll be all right when I have that.'* But, of course, nothing can ever satisfy, because what is actually being yearned for is not being addressed. This process of transferring can itself be very painful, both for the child himself and the people who care for him, who never see the child in a state of satisfaction.

Some children, when helped, can speak so movingly about how they long for a cuddle from the very person they have lost, how they long to touch her hair again, take her hand, tell her about what happened to them at school that day. For these children, the pain of the absence of the loved one is awful. They can find it so difficult to think of anything except the person who has left.

Separations from parents can also lead to the most agonising of yearning. As Bowlby (founder of attachment theory) notes:

During the second year of life there is no lack of records of children left in hospital or nursery watching the door through which a parent has departed and doing so persistently for several days in the evident hope of seeing him or her return through it.
(Bowlby, 1973)

Much of the thoughts of a child who has lost a loved one are dominated by the person he lost, memories, wishes, perceptions – he becomes mentally preoccupied with his lost love. The child finds constant reminders and references to the lost person everywhere.

A child may have comforting night-time dreams of being with the lost loved one again, of a reunion; on waking, he has the pain of realising this dream is not reality. Or suddenly, out of the blue – while eating an ice cream, halfway through a film – reality will intrude: *'Daddy shouldn't have left,' 'I haven't got a daddy any more.'*

C.S. Lewis talked of his mental preoccupation with his dead wife:

Thought after thought, feeling after feeling, action after action, had H for their object. So many roads lead through to H. I set out on one of them. But now there's an impassable frontier-post across it. So many roads once; now so many cul-de-sacs.
(Lewis, 1966)

Anton, aged six

Anton was six when his mother died. At school, he kept watching the door. When asked why, he said, *'In case my mummy comes back from heaven and walks into the room again.'* He knew about the finality of death, and yet the strength of his desperate hope and longing meant he could not let go of the hope that she would return.

Tao, aged twelve

When Tao's dad left his wife to work abroad, Tao, who adored his dad, kept commenting on people in the street who looked like Daddy, people who talked like Daddy, had a car like his, a hat like his, were playing his favourite music on their car radio, had a shirt which was Dad's favourite colour. So, the world for Tao was perceived as one huge reminder of the daddy he has lost. It can seem that there is no relief from it.

How you can help

1) **Say, to a child who has become locked into searching behaviour:**

    When people lose someone they love, it is very natural for them to try to find them, to search for them, to look for them even when they know they will never find them again. It is very natural to think you see them in the street when you know they are never coming back. It is natural to have a searching dream and to get very upset indeed when you lose a toy or something else precious to you gets lost or damaged. This is your mind's way of trying to search for your lost one, but it can get a bit muddled up for a while. So, it's just fine to let yourself feel the pain and the searching and the longing. Just find someone who can hear your pain and help comfort you.

2) **Give the child quality time to speak at length (through words and images) of the terrible pain** of the yearning, missing and searching, and to grieve (if a death) of no more shared times together, and to feel the anger and to protest about what has happened. When a child works through his grief, it is about *'summoning up reminders of the dead parent and grieving for them one by one'* (Harris-Hendriks et al., 1993).

3) **Ensure the child has time to reminisce with an emotionally available adult and tell of the lovely precious shared times**. This is about being able to linger over memories and celebrate the lovely times with an adult who is good at listening to times of joy and fun. It is vital that you listen in a free, totally noncritical way and really meet the child in his joy or delight, rather than seeming bland or giving a dulled response. The latter would be a misattunement. If the child senses that his positive feelings about his beloved lost person are not met in an affirming way, he will close down. This is because, in many ways, it is just as courageous to talk about precious, lovely and intimate moments in life as it is to talk about the painful ones. On the same

lines, make sure that if you do ask a question, it is only to inform your affirming response – *'Wow, that sounds amazing!'* Don't ask questions that are not followed by responses that meet the child in his joy state.

4) **Tell the child that these memories are priceless and will go on nourishing him throughout his life**. And that no one can ever take them away. They are a special treasure in his mind.

Helping grieving children with their feelings of despair/withdrawal and hopelessness

Despair is particularly prevalent in children who have no other person to whom they want to go for comfort. Sometimes the despair is particularly focused on the fact that the very person they need to comfort them is the one who has left them.

Despair happens when the loss has left the child with these vital unmet human needs, based on Maslow's (1943) hierarchy of needs:

Need to feel you matter (so feeling worthless, shame, social defeat).

Need for love and belonging (so feeling isolated, lonely, alienated, rejected, unwanted).

Need to feel psychologically safe in the world (so feelings psychologically unsafe in the world).

Need for meaning (so feeling hopeless and that your life is without meaning).

Some children who feel despair/hopeless after a traumatic loss have erratic changes of mood states/hope interspersed with hopelessness. For example, they think *'Daddy will come back'* or *'I'll meet Daddy again in heaven'*, and then *'I have lost Daddy for ever.'* Or they suddenly shift from sadness to anger and vice versa, for example taking photos of Daddy to bed with them one night and tearing the photos up the next day. Wanting to remember, then wanting to forget; loving Daddy, then hating him for going.

Some children withdraw from the world of people after losing someone they love and then end up feeling lost, alienated, hopeless and despairing. This is because, whether we like it or not, we are genetically programmed to meet people. Loneliness is as bad as smoking 15 cigarettes a day (Holt-Lunstad et al., 2015).

It is as if many of these children feel that the world has let them down so badly that they are compelled to move into a private, unpeopled world. Some of these children feel so betrayed by this terrible life event of tragic loss that they no longer wish to take part in an active social world. These are the children who then become hard to connect with and difficult to reach in any meaningful way. They seek neither help nor comfort. These 'lost' children can be drawn to places of desolation: an empty room, a piece of wasteland.

Bleak places become a kind of sanctuary for them; they are comforted by having an external mirror of what they feel inside.

By way of comparison, Jane Goodall found, in her moving study of chimpanzees (1990), that if young chimps lose their mothers, many cannot survive the trauma and actually die. They are old enough to survive physiologically, but they go into terrible states of despair and stop eating. There is a tragic photo of chimpanzee 'Flint', whose mother died when he was just eight years old. After his mother's death, Flint just lay down where his mother had died, and then after a few days died there himself. This is a very sobering lesson for anyone who makes light of a bereaved child's pain.

How you can help

1) **Stay with the child's feelings, however painful, without moving into platitudes or giving advice**. If the child is finding it difficult to speak literally about his feelings of hopelessness and despair, enable him to speak in images and metaphors. See the worksheets in Chapter 3, which are designed to be non-threatening for the child suffering from loss in this way. Advice and platitudes would block any desire the child

had to speak about his loss. More than anything, the question here is whether you can bear the pain in the room. *'If you wish me to weep, you yourself must first feel grief'* (Horace, 65 BC to 8 BC). You need the capacity to listen without desensitising, dodging, deflecting. It's so hard to be with a child's despair and hopelessness without moving into reassurances. But the latter never reassure a child who is in despair. The child's finding hope again is from you bearing their pain and finding the words to say that you understand. If you, as facilitator, are blocked around your own experiences of loss, then the child will pick this up on a subliminal level and not want to share much with you. Despite your best efforts, if you are blocked on grief, your voice and your empathy will come out wrongly. You will not be able to feel their pain if you are cut off from your own. Furthermore, facilitators who have undergone extensive personal therapy and have processed their own painful losses will not be afraid of the child's despair. They will be able to bear the pain in the room.

2) **Help the child to speak about what it was like to feel loved and to love this person**. Not speaking about this renders the child emotionally poorer. His love needs a voice, just as much as his pain. (See Chapter 3, the exercise called 'Festival of Moments' on the importance of reminiscence.)

3) **Express important psychological messages for children to hear when loss has moved into hopelessness/despair**. Obviously, timing is of the essence. The messages should never be used as a way for the practitioner to dodge being with the child's pain.

When you lose someone you love, it can make you hate your life, it can feel like the world has lost all its warmth and colour and has become a cold, bleak winter. But it's like the weather – feelings and emotions cannot stand still. So, with time, the warmth and colour will return.

'Comforter, where, where is your comforting?' (Hopkins, 1985, p. 61). *'There are always kind people who can comfort you. Sometimes it is just a question of finding one.'* Children are often clever at working out who is kind and who is not, who is good at understanding very painful sadness and who is not.

On the subject of crying: words of permission

'It is very natural to want to cry and cry. Some people talk of "crying a river" when they lose someone they love.'

'It is very brave to cry on the outside as well as on the inside.'

When the person deeply loved the person they lost

'When someone has deeply loved another person, it is often because they felt very seen by the person they loved, very known, and loved for who they were. Is that true for you?'

'When someone has deeply loved another person, it is often because they felt they could be themselves with this person, without having to try to be someone else. Is that true for you?'

'When someone has deeply loved another person, it is often because the loved person brought out something very alive in them. Is that true for you?'

'When someone has deeply loved another person, it is often because they feel very seen and understood and very valued by that person – very special. Is that true for you?'

For older children, if appropriate, you might give them these quotes

'We grieve most when we lose those who have helped us to thrive.' (Panksepp, 1998)

'One part of ourselves that we cherish is the wealth we have . . . from our relationships to people, for these . . . have become an inner possession.' (Klein, 1997)

'A soul mate is someone to whom we feel profoundly connected . . . This kind of relationship is so important to the soul that many have said there is nothing more precious in life.' (Moore, 1992, p. xviii)

An example of addressing a child's despair and hopelessness in sandplay therapy and having this witnessed and understood by the emotionally available adult was key

Peter, aged 13

When Peter was 11, his single mother went to prison and, because there were no other relatives to help, Peter went into residential care. His mother said she needed time not seeing her son in order to build herself up again and come off drugs. Peter took this as a personal rejection by his mother, whom he adored.

When the therapist started to work with Peter in therapy, his first images in sandplay depicted one parched landscape after another. They all evoked the most painful emotional impoverishment. Animals that Peter identified with could not get to the one solitary waterhole or were left feeding out of rubbish bins on other people's leftovers. People died of the cold, lonely and forgotten. Peter, like so many grieving children, found some tangible relief in being able to convey his inner world of anguish and despair in an art image. It helped Peter to share the barrenness and emptiness of his inner world, rather than continuing with his previous loneliness and carrying this terrible burden of pain, unshared, unconveyed. His despair, as it is for so many, was all about the agonising loss of human connection. Peter once made up an amazing story about a baby left in a place of leafless trees, stripped bare of life. Depicting this horrendous emotional lack so well, and how bleak the world became when he lost his wife, C.S. Lewis said, *'Her absence is like the sky, spread over everything'* (1966).

Gradually, Peter moved from despair to anger with his mother, and with psychoeducation realised he should not take her not wanting to see him as 'truth' about his unlovability. Peter did find a warm, kind world, just not with his mother, but in the excellent therapeutic community. He is an adult now and doing well.

2. Helping grieving children who defend against feeling their painful feelings

Defences aim to keep painful feelings out of conscious awareness. In other words, we use defences to numb emotional pain and/or to deflect from it and bring the focus onto something or someone else. Defences are formed out of conscious awareness. They are never a conscious choice. To bring this point home, think of the absurdity of a child thinking: *'To protect myself from feeling this awful loss, I will choose phobia. No, wait – obsessive compulsive rituals. No, wait – to be angry all the time.'*

We start to defend against our painful feelings when we deem them too frightening to acknowledge. They offer us ways of coping with overwhelming feelings when no one has been there to help us feel them, think about them, and make sense of them.

The trouble is that defences bring their own pain, and often a worse pain than the pain they are protecting us from. Defences often impact badly on the body, too. As Bessel van der Kolk, in the title of his book on unprocessed trauma, says, *The Body Keeps the Score* (van der Kolk, 2015). This means that the child who is defending against the pain of his loss can end up battling bodily hyperarousal, leading to all manner of physical symptoms – headaches, skin conditions, etc. And it doesn't stop at night, hence trouble sleeping or getting to sleep is common with children who are defending against a traumatic loss.

The thing is that just like an untreated physical wound, untreated emotional pain does *not* ease over time. If no one helps the child address the underlying cause of his distress, the painful memory of what happened doesn't sit nicely and quietly in a neat pocket of his mind. Instead, the pain continues, despite the protection of the defence.

Then, additional to all this, the pain from the defence that is supposed to be protecting the child from the original painful life event can last for years. I know people, for example, who have suffered from obsessive compulsive rituals for over 30 years. It truly blights a life. But it doesn't need to be this way.

All the following are defences that children I have worked with have adopted to defend against the pain of traumatic loss:

- Hypervigilance
- Panic/phobias
- Insomnia
- Amnesia
- Hearing voices
- Dissociation
- Nightmares
- Emotional numbing
- Denying what has happened
- Intellectualisation (avoiding feelings and bodily sensations and retreating into just thinking)
- Self-injury
- Self-neglect
- Bingeing, self-starvation, over-eating
- Self-silencing
- Carrying out rituals and other safety behaviours
- Holding unusual beliefs
- Avoidance
- Using drugs/alcohol/smoking to dull the pain
- Anger/rage/violence
- Relational strategies: rejection/blocked trust/maintaining emotional distance
- Separation distress/clinging (post infant stage)
- Somatisation: skin conditions, tummy aches, headaches, dizziness, etc.
- Behaviours that challenge ('I behave my trauma because no one has helped me reflect on it')

As has been said, defences have a big cost to quality of life. You choose them to protect you from pain, but they cause you pain. It's utterly miserable, for example, for a child to have to avoid the cracks in the pavement every time he goes out, or to wash his hands endlessly for those 'germs,' or to not be able to sleep night after night or to dare not go out in case he is sick in public (emetophobia).

This chapter is all about the common defences that children use against traumatic loss. Then it addresses how to gently, safely, and when the child is ready, be alongside him while he dares to feel his core feelings of traumatic loss. This way, he no longer needs his defences, as the feelings he has been defending against are no longer seen as dangerous, overwhelming, unthinkable. As Heather Geddes says, the therapist is there to help the child move *'from unbearable feelings to thinkable thoughts.'*

Helping grieving children who cut off from their grief because it is too painful

'So quickly, so quickly, the English stop speaking of grief.' (Byatt, 1995)

'Ah well, best move on now.'

'No point dwelling on the past.'

'I didn't really need Daddy anyway.'

'I don't feel anything about his going away. I've never cried about it.'

> *'Her cat had died but she had felt indifferent about it. As she had then explained: "If I let it hurt me, I'd be saddened by everything."'* (Bowlby, 1988)

Some children cannot bear to feel their grief. It is too painful and too frightening in its intensity. Defending against grief means they do not have to feel the whole host of often intensely painful, complex, disturbing feelings involved in grieving an awful loss or separation.

The two key ways to cut off from feelings of loss are, first, to cut off from memories of the person and, secondly, to cut off from feelings about that person. In other words, first the child doesn't let himself register that this person mattered deeply to him. For example, Jamie, aged eight, who loved his mother deeply, said after her death: *'Well, we all have to die some time.'* Then the child does not let himself register the *full* shock, the *full* impact of it, the *depth* of his pain, diminishing its impact on him. As Tanayah, aged eight, said, *'It's OK that Dad has gone to live with another woman who has children around our age.'* In particular, children who have been brought up to 'put their best foot forward' or to think 'big boys don't cry' can suffer from this. Also, cutting off in this way is particularly prevalent in situations where a child's parent has left or died, and he sees his other parent dealing with the loss in a cut-off way.

It is well documented in the animal kingdom that when an infant mammal loses its mother, it protests (by crying); then, if those cries are not heard, it falls into despair and then detachment. Bowlby, the founder of attachment theory, found this progression entirely replicated in situations of infants in the 1950s and 1960s who were sent to residential nurseries when their mothers went into hospital to have a baby. He wrote in 1988,

> *Infants, when looked after for too long by strange people in a strange place . . . with no one person to act as a mother-substitute, come in time to act as if neither mothering nor contact with humans have much significance. As his caretakers come and go, he ceases to attach himself to anyone, and after his return home stays remote from his parents for days.*
>
> (Bowlby, 1988)

Some bereaved children are numb for years, others for the rest of their life. If the latter happens, the quality of the child's intimate relationships will always suffer markedly.

Sometimes, cutting off results from feeling hugely hurt by a parent leaving due to an acrimonious separation and divorce or by taking his or her own life. With the latter, perhaps the parent promised to take the child on visits and hold birthday celebrations and then doesn't. It is entirely understandable for children to harden their hearts when this happens and/or cut off from their distress, pain and huge disappointment.

Because the pain of losing someone you love hurts so much, some children and some grown-ups try not to feel it at all. But that causes all sorts of problems, as shown below.

The price of cutting off

- The unbearable can very easily become the unthinkable, which again comes at a cost: a sense of nameless dread coupled with the fact that all defences bring symptoms, usually both physical and mental.
- By cutting off from so much feeling, many children cut off from their aliveness, from essential connection with themselves. As one little boy whose mother died said, *'My heart's gone in my head because I'm a weird little jelly.'* Very eloquently, he was speaking of a loss of connection with himself.
- Cutting off can be like giving yourself an anaesthetic and therefore numbing the pain. You do not feel much grief, but it can stop you feeling joy too. For some children (and adults), numbing their grief means they carry around a kind of heavy feeling all the time. This can feel miserable. By not mourning, some children become stuck, locked in their painful past that refuses to lie nicely and quietly in their mind. It is strange, but the only way for such children to move out of their pain is to move into it.
- The price for cutting off grief and all the other complex feelings that accompany it, say with parental suicide or separation/divorce, is often depression, emptiness and/or

a haunting sense of unreality at some time in life. This is because a child repressing one set of strong feelings tends to adversely affect the child's entire passionate engagement to others and to life itself. This is evident, for example, in adults who, say, have experienced life to be meaningless for years, and who, when asked whether they have ever cried for their mother (whom they loved deeply) who died when they were a child, say 'No.' In other people, however, the defence of numbing works for years, and then suddenly the person breaks down and cannot stop crying. Others live with a flatness and a narrow range of affect until they die, which protects them from addressing their grief, but the cost to their quality of life and to the quality of their relationships is considerable.

- Cutting off from your own pain often means cutting off from that of others, and hence may block your compassion and concern.
- Sadly, children who feel they can manage a traumatic loss without help all too often turn in later life to alternative 'help' and self-medication such as alcohol, over-eating, drugs, self-harm.

With his whole emotional being, it seems, a bereaved person is fighting fate, trying desperately to turn back the wheel of time and to recapture the happier days that have been suddenly taken from him. So far from facing reality and trying to come to terms with it, a bereaved person is locked in a struggle with the past.

(Bowlby, 1978)

How you can help

1) **Shakespeare wrote about Ophelia, who went mad from unaddressed grief, 'As one incapable of her own distress.' Many children who have lost someone they deeply love are incapable of their own distress too**. They need help to become capable. Without help, it is understandable that children, on some level, know that their pain is far too much and far too deep to cope with alone.

2) **When a child has cut off, we need to find the emotional meaning he attributed to the loss – often therein lies the key to open the door to their feelings**. This was the way in for Agwe, aged 10, whose mother took her own life. One day he said to his counsellor, *'She said she adored me, so how could she leave me by taking her own life if she adored me? She must have been lying all along.'* When helped by the practitioner to understand the mental states of people who take their own lives, Agwe found a way to feel his feelings both of anger and grief.

3) **Empathise with their defences.** *'No wonder you don't want to feel this. Because . . .'* Even draw walls on paper to symbolise defences. Read children the wonderful book all about this called *The Boy who Built a Wall Around Himself*, by Ali Redford.

4) **Many children who cut off from feelings of loss are in the realm of blocked trust and avoidant attachment – they literally avoid having feelings in relationships**. This is because when this child did cry out as a baby or express his feelings with a parent, he felt worse off for doing so, not better. Instead of feeling contained, soothed and empathised with, the child experienced a response which was shaming, belittling, ignoring or painful in other ways. So, before the child opens up to you, it is vital you empathise, attune and show unconditional positive regard. This way, over time, he will hopefully move from blocked trust to trust and realise that opening up to you with his feelings is safe and brings relief. Over time, through all your understanding and empathy and non-shaming talk about the painful time, you can make it safe enough for the child to move from blocked trust to trust.

5) **The child may well be alexithymic (unable to put feelings into words), so use a rich language of feelings or use emotion cards, for example, The Emotion cards or The Relationship cards** (by the authors and all available on Amazon). Use cards that convey shock, anger, helplessness. Research shows that your ability to mentalise (to feel and think about the child's mental states) will support them over time to express their feelings and so alleviate their alexithymia. Read them therapeutic stories about loss, such as *The Day the Sea Went Out and Never Came Back* (which I wrote).

6) **If the child is cut off from grief due to underlying hurt, I suggest the exercise, Museum of Hurt (see Chapter 3)**.

Helping grieving children who bottle up their feelings and put on a happy face

Give sorrow words: the grief that does not speak, whispers the o'er fraught heart and bids it breaks.

(Shakespeare, Macbeth, 4.3.209–10)

Children who bottle up their feelings have not cut off from grief: they feel it intensely, but just on the inside not on the outside. Some children who look as if they are coping well with the death or permanent departure of a parent, or a separation/divorce, or a school move that resulted in the loss of a best friend they had known for years are weeping quietly inside.

Research shows that grief left unspoken, bottled up inside, can lead to both mental and physical ill-health. As mentioned earlier, one longitudinal study shockingly found that people who bottled up their emotions increased their risk of cancer by 70 per cent and increased their chance of premature death from all causes by more than 30 per cent (Chapman et al., 2013).

Some children bottle up their feelings of grief because they sense that their parent is struggling emotionally. So, the child decides that there is no space in his mind for him to have grief as well. In fact, he may have fantasies that if he were to cry or shake or say how much he was hurting inside, the parent would fall apart, or get angry. In psychology circles, this is known as fear that a parent will collapse or retaliate. Certainly, such a child has no faith or hope whatsoever in being comforted. Sometimes the child is spot-on in this appraisal of his parent being fragile and vulnerable. Other times he is way off – he is projecting onto his parent his own feelings that *he* might fall apart completely if he let himself cry. In such cases, his protection is not helping anyone, especially himself. Such a child needs his parent to raise the subject, to empathise, to say, *'I can imagine you feel such pain about . . .'* to show him he is emotionally strong enough to talk about the loss.

Sometimes the boot is on the other foot: the parent tries to protect the child by not talking about her own and the child's loss. This parent is actually only protecting herself. Nobody talking about the loss can actually inhibit or prevent the child's mourning process. In contrast, if a parent is in deep distress, in terms of loud howling, then a child may feel frightened by the intensity of this and so definitely will bottle up his own feelings. But a parent shedding tears is a real model of how to express feelings and the importance of not bottling them up.

How you can help

1) **Children who bottle up their feelings need role models of adults who can talk about the pain of grief as safe and natural.** It is unhelpful for the child who bottles up his feelings to be around adults who are bottling up theirs. It can be helpful for these children to see grieving adults cry, in order to feel 'permission' to express their own grief.
2) **Children need to know that it is healthy and natural after a shock to sob loudly and shake or scream, and that bottling up feelings can be damaging.** Freud knew this. He said,

> *It is of great consequence whether there was an energetic reaction to the [emotional] experience. By reaction we here understand a whole series of voluntary or involuntary [responses; e.g. crying/shaking] through which according to experience [emotions] are discharged. If the success of the reaction is of sufficient strength it results in the disappearance of a great part of the affect. Language attests to this fact of daily observation in such expressions as "to give vent to one's feelings" to be "relieved by weeping" etc. If the reaction is suppressed, the affect remains united with the memory.*
>
> (Freud, 1909)

If the reaction is suppressed, meaning grief is bottled up or avoided, the affect (emotion) *'remains united with the memory'*. This means the child can be haunted by the traumatic memory, with all manner of fallout in terms of debilitating mental and physical health problems.

If a child who bottles up his feelings is to let go of them, he needs to be with someone with whom he feels safe – someone he knows intuitively is comfortable with his expression of grief, who will not pull away from it or try to distract him into happier feelings. As Bowlby (1973) said, *'We can only really mourn in the presence of another.'* This is such a true statement, and particularly for children. Many children who bottle up have a sense that feelings are just too strong to unleash on their own, and besides doing so alone is far too lonely. When children like this find someone with whom they feel psychologically safe and who they trust, one day the dam breaks. They start to sob and sob. The relief and gratitude can be enormous at least to feel peace in their body and mind.

Helping grieving children who have moved into defensive anger

> *'Anger was an easier coat to wear.'* (Mark Johnson, author of the book *Wasted: Violence, Addiction – and Hope*)

Some children who have suffered a traumatic loss move into anger. As a consequence, many get into trouble at home and/or at school. Some lose good friends as well, so they have even more loss to deal with (or to avoid dealing with). Anger, entirely out of conscious awareness, can be used by the child as a protection against the unbearable feelings of despair, grief and hurt. Tragically, anger used like this can all too easily turn into bitterness and a hardened heart.

There is relevant neurochemistry here that all schools should know about in order to prevent punishing grieving children. When a child loses someone he has loved deeply – someone who consistently activated natural opioids in his brain – he is left in a state of opioid withdrawal. To make matters worse, this shift in biochemistry can activate opposing neurochemical forces in the brain; this involves the release of too-high levels of a chemical called acetylcholine, which cascades over the higher brain and can make people feel angry or hostile. At optimal levels, acetylcholine can help people concentrate and feel alert. But at high levels, acetylcholine can make people angry, hostile and attacking.

This neurochemical profile of low opioids and high levels of acetylcholine triggers the same reaction in other mammals. For example, with higher primates like chimpanzees who are accustomed to optimal levels of opioids. When they move into opioid withdrawal from an experience of loss, these animals become very nasty with each other.

Alan, aged 15, was an A-grade student. He loved his older stepbrother. One day his stepbrother was killed in a motorbike accident. Alan's behaviour at school became so violent and angry that he was temporarily excluded. Luckily, he was given a counsellor who knew about the transition from loss to anger. The counsellor's work with Alan impacted positively on Alan's neurochemical imbalance. As a result, Alan came back into mainstream school and no longer had an anger issue.

Not all children will move from traumatic loss to anger, but research shows that if you have poor frontal lobe functions and so find it hard to reflect, mentalise and calm down after stress, you are particularly vulnerable (Chester et al., 2013). This weakness is due to parents not helping the child enough to emotionally regulate through validating empathy and mental state talk (because their own parent didn't do this for them). This omission means that effective stress regulatory systems are not established in the child's brain. It is never too late for this to happen, though (that's where you come in), due to the brain's neuroplasticity.

The following neurochemical reactions can happen as a result of traumatic loss, also contributing to the triggering of anger.

- Increased activation of the brain chemical corticotrophin-releasing factor (CRF): this in turn activates high levels of stress hormones (one of which is cortisol) in the brain and body. These stress hormones can block the release of positive arousal chemicals (including dopamine, opioids, oxytocin). They also activate stress response systems in the brain, leading to depression, anxiety disorders and/or problems with aggression.
- Decreased levels of serotonin: low serotonin can increase aggressive impulses, hence some of the angry outbursts of people with broken hearts, jealous feelings or threat of loss. Monkeys who have low serotonin are impulsive and aggressive. *'Given the opportunity, they will make dangerous leaps from tree to tree that other monkeys won't attempt. They get into frequent fights'* (Kotulak, 1997). Also, due to the depletion of serotonin, (a mood stabiliser), people with poor frontal lobe functions who are suffering traumatic loss are wide open to impulsive outbursts of irritation, anger, rage or attacks on the self, as in self-harm. (Panksepp, 2004).

Schools need to be aware of these neurochemical changes in the context of children who have lost a loved one or who are 'loving in torment' at home (loving someone who is also hurting them physically, emotionally and/or sexually). Many children suffering the pain of loss or rejection behave in very angry or aggressive ways. When schools are not informed of the effects of trauma on children, it's all too easy for people to start hating these children, punishing them and wanting to exclude them, rather than offering an emotionally available adult. The hope is that increasing staff awareness on the neurochemical changes resulting from traumatic loss will improve levels of compassion in the staff, so children are helped at school instead of being excluded.

How you can help

1) **When children move into anger to protect themselves from the pain of grief and hurt, as Dan Hughes (a child clinical psychologist) says, 'Angry children need help to feel sad.'** In other words, we need to help them to feel psychologically safe enough with us in order to feel their pain rather than defend against their pain. We need to have faith in the power of our empathy, compassion and understanding to help them to dare to feel sad. Otherwise, as Sasha Baron Neulinger (2021) says, *'By not allowing yourself to feel, you remain a prisoner of your own pain.'* One thing you can say to the child locked in anger is, *'I can really hear how angry you are. I really get that. And I am also wondered if another part of you is really hurting bout it too.'*

2) **The comforting (particularly physical comforting) of a grieving child who has become angry (due to the neurochemical changes detailed above) will release natural calming opioids in his brain, coupled with the lovely emotion chemical oxytocin.** These will bring down to base rate those too-high levels of acetylcholine. As Panksepp and Biven (1998) say, *'Both opioids and oxytocin are powerful anti-aggressive molecules, and they also have a powerful inhibitory effect on separation distress.'*

3) **With older children, you may like to consider explaining the brain chemistry shift from loss to anger**. For example, Koya lost her mother when she was 13. She then got involved in county lines just to get love and affection. She ended up in a juvenile detention centre. Unprovoked by any obvious incident, she kept smashing up her television set. She had no idea why she did it, nor did the prison officers. She thought she was just mad. It added yet more pain to her already desperately low self-esteem.

It was really helpful, therefore, when the prison counsellor explained about the neurochemistry of grief and the shift from loss to anger. With the help of her counsellor, Koya began to mourn her mother for the first time. After that she was no longer angry. The comfort she received whilst mourning had released calming chemicals and brought her acetylcholine down to base rate. It is not hard to see that if a grieving child has no person to turn to for comfort, then he can have no neurochemical brakes on the aggressive behaviour that so often is the legacy of uncomforted grief.

4) **Some children need to know about the importance of healthy anger towards the person who has gone (even if that person is dead), rather than thinking that their anger is just plain wrong**. Many children do not know that anger is a healthy protest against the trauma of the loss – it is anger at the pain they have been left to feel. In other words, when you lose someone you love, it is perfectly natural to feel anger towards them – 'How dare you leave me!' This 'healthy anger' is different from anger as a defence against the pain, which means being angry at everyone and everything (as described in point 3 above), the sort that gets you in real trouble at school; anger directed towards the person or situation of loss helps enormously in the recovery process. Children need to know that they are not bad for feeling this; it is a part of grief. For example, Tom, aged 16, had moved into generalised anger at school after his mother died. He had multiple detentions as a result. Then, with his counsellor, he was able to direct his anger in a healthy way. He drew a picture of cancer and scribbled it all out with large black pens – 'How dare cancer take my mother! I hate cancer. I hate this life without my mum.'

5) **Children can be helped to understand what is happening when the surviving parent gets all their anger**. If the child is old enough to understand, you might like to explain how, in order to keep the person who has gone or died as totally good in their mind, they are angry with the surviving parent instead. They need help to redirect their anger towards the person who has left, even if that parent left due to terminal illness. Support a healthy protest. Model it: '*So, Tom, as well as being angry at your father (who is still alive), I wonder if a part of you is furious (and it doesn't have to be rational) at your mum for getting cancer and dying.*' Tom managed to do this. He put a puppet on the chair to represent his mum.

Counsellor: '*So talk to your mum as if she were here, Tom, and don't worry about being rational; say anything you want. Finish this sentence: "Mum . . . what I want you to know is . . ."*'

Tom: '*I really trusted you, Mum, to stay around. You left. You shouldn't have got cancer. You should have been weller. You should have got more check-ups. I hate you for leaving me.*'

Tom's speaking so honestly about his core anger then opened up his heart to feeling his core grief, and he was able to sob with the counsellor for the first time.

Helping children whose defence against the pain of traumatic loss has resulted in anxiety

When children find the pain of traumatic loss intolerable to feel and think about, they may end up defending against it in ways that leave them with ongoing anxiety – feelings of nameless dread, a strong belief that something awful will happen in the future to them or to someone/the people they love (but they don't know what). Anxiety is often then accompanied with physical complaints, hypervigilance, avoidance of situations where they believe the feared awful event might happen, rumination and catastrophising thoughts.

Additionally, for some children who suffer from anxiety, losing relatively minor things – for example, losing their dummy or fluffy toy cat – may bring on terrible feelings of panic. The child may develop obsessional checking rituals and get very distressed if his favourite teddy is not in its exact place sitting at the exact angle they need it to be. Others adopt a defence known as *displacement*, which means redirecting the painful feelings about their traumatic loss onto something they see as less threatening, germs for example. So they keep washing their hands in case the awful germs cause some form of catastrophe. All the while, this is a deflection from the real underlying pain of their traumatic loss. Other common signs of anxiety in children and young people are panic attacks, phobias, fear of dying, fear of going mad, fear of losing control, fear that a member of your family is going to die. With any of the above, your mind is not a nice place to be.

Healthy fear is *present* focused and short lived because you do something to alleviate it. In contrast, anxiety is *future* focused because it's about an expected horrible event in the future that you have no control over (Sylvers et al., 2011). With anxiety there is no immediate threat and yet the child still feels very afraid all the time. This is a terribly painful way to live life; as the poet Les Murray says, '*The blow that never falls batters you stupid*' (Murray, 1997).

This painful way of being in the world can go on for years. In fact, without therapeutic intervention, it often blights lives for decades. I know many people who have suffered from obsessive compulsive disorder (OCD) or panic attacks or phobias for decades. All have a loss or trauma that they have never really processed.

More about anxiety as a defence against the pain of traumatic loss

Anxiety is a coping mechanism, just one of the ways that the mind tries to protect the child from having to face and feel his traumatic loss, but it brings its own terrible pain and anguish. Treating the symptoms of anxiety never gets to the cause. So even if one symptom goes away through behaviour modification or desensitisation techniques, another anxiety symptom will, at some point, come in its place *unless* you address the cause. It's vital that the cause is addressed before the teenage years, when hormonal changes often mean that defences that might have been serving a child well pre-puberty, just don't hold any more. Hence *50 per cent of mental health problems start by age 14, and 75 per cent by age 24* (www.mentalhealth.org.uk/statistics/mental-health-statistics-children-and-young-people).

As with all defence mechanisms, the child is not aware that his mind is protecting him from pain in this way. He just knows he feels anxious; period. He has no idea that what happened in the past (namely the traumatic loss), rather than sitting nicely in the unconscious depths of his mind, is continuing on a daily basis to colour his perception with dread. The child has no idea that what he fears in the future has actually happened in the past. In other words, at the time of the traumatic loss, there was a death of the world as he knew it – a catastrophic shock, a total feeling of loss of control. And no one was there to help him with all this. In effect, the child is trying to prevent a loss in the future that has already happened in the past. As Gabor Maté, a famous psychologist, says, '*Anxiety is the cry of some desperate childhood part of themselves for help.*' We need to '*learn to get help with that part. Anxiety can be relived and recovered from if we look at the source*' (Maté, 2019).

How you can help

1) **Form a safe working alliance with a child/teenager**, enabling them to feel psychologically safe enough with you to want to talk about past life events that were very frightening and which are fuelling their anxiety today. Explain how we often fear in the future what happened in the past.

2) **Help the child to feel safe enough, when he is ready, and without any pressure, to tell the story of his loss**. '*By not allowing yourself to feel, you remain a prisoner of your own pain*' (Neulinger, 2021). Anxiety is so often the consequence of 'un-storied emotions.' The child often needs help to find his narrative contextualisation of his current fears. If the child has moved into anxiety, it is highly unlikely that he ever told his story of loss to someone who could really listen and help him process, work through, and properly grieve what happened. As Angus and Greenberg (2011) state, '*We cannot leave a place until we have first arrived*,' meaning that we cannot let go of anxiety until we go to the 'place' of the core painful life experience fuelling the anxiety. In short, anxiety is a defence against painful feelings that are seen as too dangerous to feel.

But when those feelings are felt and thought about and expressed in a safe therapeutic context, the defence of anxiety is no longer needed.

3) **Know how children heal**. Richard Lane and Leslie Greenberg (the latter is the founder of emotion focused therapy) conducted research on what people who suffer from neurotic anxiety need to do to heal. They found that people need to get to the core feelings underneath their defences. As Greenberg says, *'We cannot live an anxiety-free life until we get to the core feelings underneath.'* (Angus and Greenberg, 2011). They found that people heal if they *change emotion with emotion*. This means changing neurotic or maladaptive emotion (such as anxiety or catastrophising) to healthy core feelings such as empowered anger and grief (Lane et al., 2015). Having done this, people could then live their lives free of the blight of ongoing anxiety and/or depression. It is exactly the same with children. We need to help them move from anxiety to empowered anger and grief. Empowered anger is not anger that blames, but owned anger. For example: *'I feel so angry that cancer took my mum. I hate cancer SO much,'* said Sophia, aged 7. Then Tom aged 11, *'I hate my Dad for going away and I also love him. But sometimes the hate smashes up the love.'* He said this when he had accessed his anger after living for three years with anxious ruminations. The latter dissipated after he found and expressed his empowered anger witnessed by his excellent practitioner.

Children and teenagers who suffer from anxiety need to know that frightening events in their life that have never been properly talked about with an emotionally available adult are a common cause of anxiety. You might:

- Whilst drawing on a whiteboard or paper to make your words come to life, say something like this: *'When something frightening happens in our lives, it can feel like our whole world has become unsafe [use age-appropriate language]. You can see the world as full of threats, because a very big threat DID happen that might make you feel that things like that will just happen again. If, with my help, you can think about what shook your belief in the world being a safe place, then it's like taming a lion. The lion will stop roaring at you all the time (your anxiety) and you won't keep seeing threat everywhere.'*
- Find the words to say that once they are helped by you to grieve the original loss, it renders the traumatic memory bearable as opposed to catastrophic, and so they no longer need their anxious thoughts as protection against that memory. (It's actually called memory reconsolidation, but they don't need to know this.)
- Say that *'Anxiety is a normal response to what naturally happened to you'* Gabor Maté (2019). Then help them to know that talking about what happened with someone like you, who is trained to listen well and help them make sense of what happened and finding their anger about it and feeling their grief about it, can lead to an anxiety free life.

Bringing it all together

All we have written in this chapter about how children heal from traumatic loss, is entirely in line with the research endorsed by the established top experts in the field of trauma, namely Judith Herman (2002) and Bessel Van der Kolk (2015, 2021). They both agree on the following three stages of recovery, which I have adapted for work with children and young people as follows.

Stage One: Establishing safety.

Regaining a sense of psychological safety through relationship with you as practitioner coupled with physiologically calming interventions, e.g. attachment play, mindfulness, use of your compassionate voice and empathic words. Unless the child is emotionally regulated and feels really safe with you, reflective time with you about their loss, is unlikely to be effective or effective enough.

Stage Two: Retelling the story of the painful loss/traumatic event. Grieving.

The child tells you the story of their painful loss through collaborative sense-making with the support of art media, imagery, emotion cards, emotion worksheets (see Chapter 3). Any negative self-referencing beliefs, e.g. *'It was my fault that my parents split up. It was my fault that Mummy got sick,'* are challenged. In this stage the child feels safe enough to grieve in your presence.

Stage Three: Empowerment and taking control. Reconnecting with others and with ordinary life.

> *The essential features of psychological trauma are disempowerment and disconnection from others. The recovery process therefore is to restore power and control to the survivor and [bring connection]. Many well-intentioned attempts to assist the person, founder, because this fundamental principle of empowerment is not observed. Recovery can take place only within the context of relationships; it cannot occur in isolation.*
>
> (Herman, 2002)

Of course, when the child feels empowered anger, is enabled to truly grieve, and has you as an emotionally available adult to help him make sense of what has happened, this *is* empowerment. But there is another form of taking control, namely when you help the child put feelings into words, images or artistic form, whether a poem, a drawing or a sandplay. So, the whole of the next chapter is dedicated to this. But before you go there, here are some vital quotations that underline this point:

Carl Jung the famous psychoanalyst says,

To the extent that I managed to translate the emotions into images – that is to say, to find images which were concealed in the emotions I was inwardly calmed and reassured. Had I left those images hidden in the emotions, I might have been torn to pieces by them.

(Carl Jung, 1928)

Kate Clanchy ran many poetry groups in schools where she enabled hundreds of young people to bring poetic form to some of their most painful feelings about traumatic loss. She states,

My students are gaining control over a torrent of experience that has rendered them powerless. And if they dig deep, and find effective images, [or] make a good poem out of the truths of their lives, then that is not just control, but power.

(Kate Clanchy, 2019)

Here is an example from a teenager Kate Clanchy worked with who had lost both her parents to drug addiction:

So what does it feel like to lose your father to heroin, Amiee? Like being an out of control car, a broken branch on the ground, like rubbish that seagulls are picking, says Amiee. And when, after that, your sister leaves home? Like the moment the cloud goes over the sun and your room is full of shadow. And what does death look like? Like your mum's addict boyfriend, coming to call with a can of Stella, like the stairwell you were too young to fling him down. And where is your mother, now Amiee? In my room. In the sunset. In her scent. In my poem, Miss, safe.

(Kate Clanchy, 2019)

So we will finish with the profound images and 'taking control' from three children who found images to bring form to their grief and were empowered in their process of recovery by doing so.

Bembe, aged seven, drew his depressed, emotionally unavailable father as a patch of fog.

Helping grieving children who defend against feeling their painful feelings

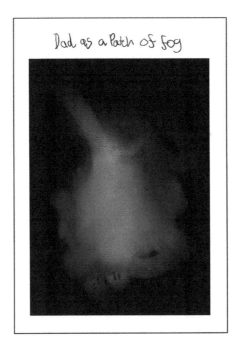

Chantale, aged eight drew her dead Mummy as just a speck on the horizon.

Sophie, aged eleven who lost her mum to cancer drew 'the mum in my mind' as a lovely soft pillow.

3. Practical ways of enabling children to speak about and work through feelings of loss

The exercises in this chapter are designed to support children who have experienced a painful loss. The exercises are designed to help them grieve, to make sense of what has happened and enable them to heal without the loss haunting their life as an unresolved trauma. The exercises also aim to provide a whole host of ideas to enable children to speak about their loss in unthreatening, supportive ways.

Children need help with a language for grief, as do so many adults! So, the exercises also enable children to speak about their grief and loss, using the images provided, when everyday words so often fail to do justice to what they feel. The exercises can help children to speak about the subtle nuances, the intensity and the specific meaning of their painful life experiences. In turn this enables the practitioner to help them make that vital shift from 'un-storied' emotions (emotions that are disturbing and frightened as they lack narrative contextualisation) to forming a coherent narrative for what has happened. This means the child moves from negative self-referencing, *'what happened was my fault,'* to being able to stand back, see what happened far more objectively and develop self-compassion.

The exercises allow ease and flow to the conversation between practitioner and child. They empower the child to show, enact, draw their feelings often with real emotional clarity and depth. Additionally, many of the development sections in the exercises, support creative and imaginative ways of expression. There are also some tasks that just require a tick in a box, or a quick colouring-in. These are particularly useful for reluctant children or those with blocked trust who then feel an ease with participating as at the outset, not much is being asked of them.

The tasks and exercises are not designed to be worked through in chronological order. Also, there are far too many to attempt them all in one go: the child could feel bombarded. So just pick those you think would be right for the particular child you are working with, taking into account their age, and how defended or undefended they are in talking about their feelings of loss. Photocopy or download and print the appropriate exercises for your time together and have art materials nearby in case the child is willing to move freely to a deeper exploration.

Copyright material from Margot Sutherland and Nicky Armstrong (2022), *Helping Children with Loss: A Guidebook*. Routledge.
DOI: 10.4324/9781003214113-4

Practical ways of enabling children to speak about feelings of loss

Note: please feel free to change the instructions and adapt the exercises to ensure they are age appropriate

As you use the exercises, consider your language for loss, appropriate to the age and developmental level of the child. For example, by and large, children of school age can understand very well about the finality of death. They can understand that death is permanent, that the loved person will not be coming back. However, children under the age of five may believe that Daddy or Mummy has just gone to another place – for example, a cloud in the sky, heaven – and is hanging about 'up there.' They may therefore believe that death is in some way reversible, that Daddy who died will come back some day. Other under-fives are well aware that he will not. It is good to explain to younger children what death means. They can often understand things like: '*His body stopped working. When that happens, the person dies. No one can keep living without their body.*'

We also highly recommend reading to the child, if appropriate to their particular loss, the story that accompanies this book. It is called *The Day the Sea Went Out and Never Came Back.*

Shock states

Objective

So many children have no word for shock and yet they are in shock! With no name for shock, many children develop all manner of symptoms: nightmares, hypervigilance, checking rituals, phobias, behaviours that challenge. Giving them the concept of shock through images can be vital for the child to be able to move from the 'unthought known' (Bollas,1987) that is *'I know it but I've not yet had a thought about it'* to the 'thought known.' So many children are deeply relieved by this. You can then consolidate this self-knowledge with appropriate psychoeducation in terms of how they can release shock from body and mind.

Instructions to give to the child

There is all the difference in the world between being able to prepare yourself for a bad thing that you know is going to take place (for example someone you love leaving) and a bad thing happening for which you have had no warning and so it's just an awful shock. Look at the picture and think of one or more shocks you have suffered in your life. Did any of them make you feel like any of the images in the picture? If so, tick those pictures. If it's not any of these, draw your own feelings about the shock/s you have had in the empty box (use another sheet of paper if you need) and give each picture a title.

What was the worst thing for you about the shock? Write words on the shock picture that describe how you felt at the time. How do you think the shocking things that happened to you then are still affecting your life now?

Practical ways of enabling children to speak about feelings of loss

When the person you loved left or died, it can feel like a terrible shock. If this happened to you, did the shock feel like any of these? Tick or colour in one or more of the boxes if it did. If it felt like something else, draw or write what it felt like in the empty box.

Development
The shock energies

If you have musical instruments, ask the child to play the energy of the shock. If they are ready to do so, then ask them to play their protest/anger about the shock.

As shock can leave a child feeling helpless or impotent, it can be very healing to take power back in this way through drama, drums, voice, in terms of making an energised protest. As Herman (2015) a top trauma specialist says,

> The essential features of psychological trauma are disempowerment and disconnection from others. The recovery process therefore is to restore power and control to the survivor and [bring connection]. Many well-intentioned attempts to assist the person flounder, because this fundamental principle of empowerment is not observed. Recovery can take place only within the context of relationships; it cannot occur in isolation.
>
> **'When my house burnt down, I could see the rising sun' (anon)**

Obviously, this development will only be appropriate for some children in some circumstances. Molly, aged nine, for example, was heartbroken when Dad moved out and she went to live with her mother and her new partner and his children. However, her stepsister and stepbrother taught her how to fish and ice skate and windsurf, all of which she adored. Before meeting them she had always been on her iPad in her spare time.

Instructions to give to the child

With any of the shocks in your life, can you relate to the saying *'When my house burnt down, I could see the rising sun'*? If so, write down what unexpectedly good things happening/opportunities opened up to you because of the shock/loss/catastrophe that would not have come about if the awful thing hadn't happened. Because some people are taken over by the force of unmourned grief, they sometimes do not see the openings or opportunities that might come their way.

Museum of loss

Objective
The 'Make it Count' campaign found that nearly half-a-million children in the UK said they had no one to speak to at school when they were experiencing feelings of sadness or worry. As a result, many said they had sleep difficulties, tended to fight, struggled with homework and/or withdrew (Mental Health Foundation, October 2018). So this exercise is to support those vital conversations between practitioners and children where losses can really be talked about, grieved and made sense of.

As the child shows you round their museum, if they clearly feel comfortable about the task ask them how they felt about the loss after it happened and how they feel about it now. Ensure empathic statements are made in response to every loss they tell you about.

Instructions to give to the child
Think of people and places which you have lost in your life. Draw or write the losses on the various museum stands. Then, if you like, you can show me around your museum. Pick a little figure to be you and one to be me. (It's good to have small plastic figures or miniatures for this.)

Would you take me around your museum starting where you like and tell me about losses you want to talk about.

Practical ways of enabling children to speak about feelings of loss

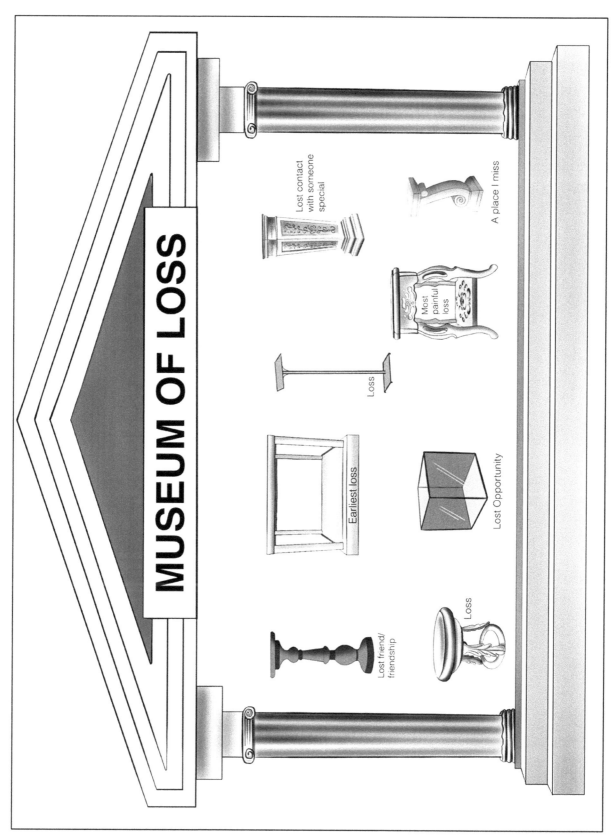

Development
Talk about the importance of reminiscence

Talk to the child about the fact that, even if they have lost the person they love, or lost their love, no one can ever take away the memories of the lovely times they had together. It is important to bring these to mind whenever you want. They can keep warming us with expansive life-energising feelings. There is neuroscience research backing for this. Namely reminiscence reduces stress chemicals in the brain and activates reward chemicals (Speer and Delgado, 2019).

When the pain of loss gets into everything

Objective

A child's life can so easily get derailed by unmourned grief, leaving them struggling emotionally, relationally, and with all the demands of school. As we have seen, loss can result in the most unbearable pain. In fact, it triggers the same centres in the brain as physical pain (Eisenberger, 2012). Also, brain research shows that blocked grief, over time, all too easily becomes depression (Panksepp and Watt, 2011).

The best way to get the train back on the tracks, so to speak, is for the child to find the courage to grieve with someone he trusts. As Bowlby (1981), originator of attachment theory, says, 'It is not possible to grieve without the presence of another.' Crying with a trusted other brings amazing relief and triggers opioids, oxytocin and the parasympathetic branch of the autonomic nervous system, particularly when new meaning comes out of collaborative sense-making about the loss. In contrast, know that crying on your own can make you feel worse not better. (Gracanin et al., 2014).

So this exercise is to support the child to think about the fallout in their life from the loss and what they need now to heal.

Instructions to give to the child

Look at the five trains in the pictures. Two are running fine, but three have been derailed by big blobs of sadness. Think of losses, longings, disappointments, the pain of being left out, feelings of not belonging, in your life that hurt such a lot that it was like they derailed you for a time. Perhaps they are still doing so.

Write on the big blobs of sadness some of those particularly painful losses that come to mind. Are some of your trucks now back on track? If so who or what helped you? If some of your trucks are still struggling to get back on track think about what you need, and from whom, to help your life run more smoothly and with more ease from now on.

Practical ways of enabling children to speak about feelings of loss

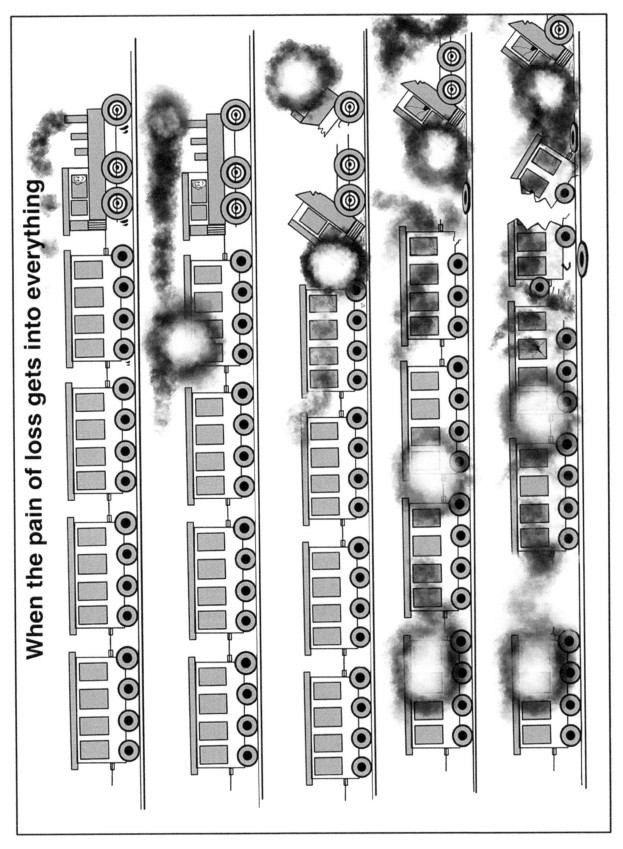

When the pain of loss gets into everything

Development

Ask the child to think of unmet emotional needs as they are always there in any painful emotional experience. So if you could have anything from anyone, what would you want for healing. If they need help, write words on a big whiteboard I need 'comfort' to 'get my self-respect back,' 'to feel very valued by someone,' 'to talk about the person I lost and the lovely things I remember about them,' 'to get angry for what happened,' 'for someone to help me take away my self-hate/my thinking I am rubbish.' You can include in this list what you believe to be the unmet emotional needs in the child you are working with.

Museum of hurt

Objective
This exercise is designed to support the child to staying open to their more vulnerable feelings of hurt so that they can start to process these feelings instead of defending against them. A wealth of research shows that the latter leads to all manner of mental and physical health problems and difficulties in relation to self and others. It is hoped that the containing function of the images will help the child to feel psychologically safe enough to do so. The importance of grieving a significant loss is recognised. Yet the major hurts in one's life also need attention too.

Instructions to give to the child
Look at each exhibit in turn. Think of times or events in your life when you felt very hurt. Choose exhibit stands in the Museum of hurt. Think of a title or phrase to describe the event and write this by the exhibit. What was the worst thing about it? What do you want the person who hurt you to know or understand? Try saying it to them now as if they were in the room.

- 'What I want you to know is . . .'
- 'I am so hurt that you . . .'
- 'I feel so angry because you . . .'

Ask the child to stand back and look at all the hurts they have entitled. Which are the most emotionally charged? Which still feel raw? Which don't seem to matter so much anymore?

Practical ways of enabling children to speak about feelings of loss

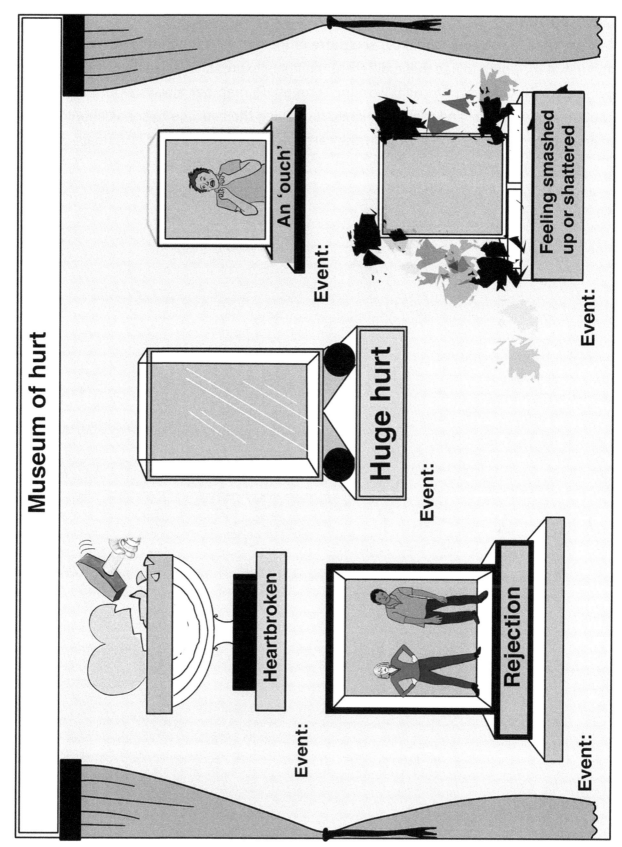

Development

Ask the child to use clay to make a sculpture of the hurt or ask them to do a sandplay about it. It may help to use these different modes of expression as each offers a different perspective and different form of working through. Remember always to empathise about the pain of hurt and praise the child for having the courage to speak about it. Lots of adults are not brave enough to say they are hurt. They just get angry instead.

Life after losing a person or their love

Objectives

When you lose a person you love, or you lose their love, someone who has been a key part of your world, the perception of many other things in your life can be dramatically affected. You can begin to look at life through spectacles coloured by desolation, hurt, pain and anger. It is vital that children work through their pain and loss in order not to suffer from depression, anxiety or ongoing bitterness.

When children who have suffered a loss, do not grieve in the presence of a comforting other, they often move from pain to emotional numbing or pain to anger or pain to anxiety. All too often this then results in them losing connection with the original source of their pain, namely their loss and instead suffering from a blighted life.

Also, grief, which is denied, unmourned or unworked through, can result in all manner of physical symptoms. In fact, hopelessness and depression are a key risk for heart disease and death (Anda et al., 1993). Sadly, people who feel they can manage without help all too often turn to alternative 'help' and self-medication, e.g. alcohol, overeating, drugs, self-harm.

So this exercise provides some language for grief, using evocative metaphors. Finding the right words and images can be a vital first step for children to begin their mourning process.

Instructions to give to the child

After a painful loss it is such a smart thing to talk to someone who is good at listening and understanding what you are going through, rather than cutting off or bottling up your feelings. Unmourned grief can all too often mess up on your enjoyment of life. Some people, including lots of adults get stuck in sadness because they have never talked about it to someone who is really good at listening and who really understands about grief.

Look at the picture. Tick any of the images that feel right for you in describing what life feels like for you without this person, and/or without their love. If none of the images are right for you, draw your own. Can you let me know what is it about the images that you have chosen that really say what you feel about this painful loss?

Practical ways of enabling children to speak about feelings of loss

Life after losing a person or their love

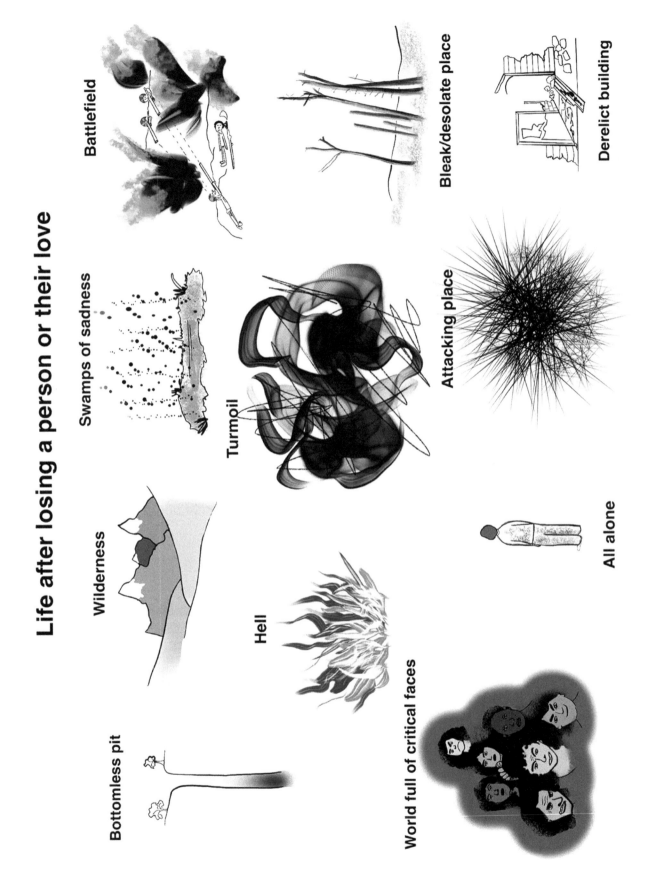

Battlefield · Bleak/desolate place · Derelict building · Swamps of sadness · Turmoil · Attacking place · Wilderness · Hell · All alone · Bottomless pit · World full of critical faces

Development

If the child has ticked bleak/desolate place ask them to draw their own bleak desolate place, or write a poem about it, or do a sandplay about it They might then want to write a letter to the person they really miss. Alternatively, you might like to ask them to finish the unfinished sentences like those below.

(Obviously just pick the ones that are right for this child and their context or write your own. These are just to give you ideas.)

What I miss about you is . . .
What I remember doing with you is . . .
What I loved about knowing you was . . .
I am angry with you because . . .
What I really miss about you is . . .
What I wish I had said to you is . . .
What I feel about myself now you are gone is . . .
What I feel about you now you are gone is . . .
What I need to you to understand is . . .

Festival of Moments: the importance of remembering and reminiscing

Objective

This exercise offers the child both the time and space to reminisce about the really good times with a person who is dead, or who is no longer in their life, or who they see all too rarely (e.g. a parent in prison, or a parent now living abroad or far away). Sharing these remembered times with someone who really listens with warmth and delight and appreciates what is being said in a free, non-judgemental way, enriches these treasured memories and imbues them with life and meaning. We know this sort of reminiscence is hugely healing. We have the neuroscientific evidence that reminiscence engages parts of the brain that are key for reward-processing and emotion regulation (Speer et al., 2017). It can also help the child understand that if he has been lucky enough to have had a profound human connection with another person, it will remain like a jewel in his memory for ever and continue to warm him deeply.

Instructions to give to the child

Think of treasured memories of special times and special moments you have with a person who really mattered to you but who you don't see any more or don't see enough. For some people those special moments are a fleeting look, or a handhold or something they said to you or a time of shared laughter, or a holiday moment with that special person you will never forget Then, write or draw these moments in the festival. Find a little object to represent yourself. Place your little object at each exhibit in turn so as to revisit and share that moment with me in the way you want to. Make sure you really take the time to fully savour those moments again, rather than just rushing on to the next exhibit.

Practical ways of enabling children to speak about feelings of loss

Development

You might like to ask the child to bring in photos that really matter to them and tell you the story of the photo. Describe their feelings and why the photo is so important to them. What does it make them feel about themselves, the people in the photo, the place in the photo?

Scrapbook of important shared places and things we did together

Objective

When we remember people in our lives who have had a huge influence on us, the places where we were with these people are often very evocative and emotionally charged for better or worse. But this exercise is looking at positive associations with places as the child is asked to remember only positive memories of the missed person here. In terms of activities, so many children who have lost a loved one really need to tell you in detail about a loved shared activity, e.g. football on a Sunday afternoon, hilarious rough and tumble, badminton in the summer sun, visiting that lovely pizza restaurant. Again, really listen and help them bring colour and vibrancy to their storytelling made all the richer by your enlivened, interested affirming response. Really listen to the child in their describing of the places. The more senses the better. What colours do they remember, smells, what did the place make them feel? Would they like to revisit these places only with the missed person or on their own without that person?

Instructions to give to the child

Think about places that you went with the person you miss and/or the things you did together. These were lovely together times that you fondly remember about your time with this person. Then write on the scrapbook the names of these places and/or things you did together. If eight boxes are not enough, that's fine, just draw more boxes. If eight is too many, just leave the ones you don't need, as blank.

Now, go back to each box that you have written in.

Write words or key phrases in each of your boxes about what was so special about this activity or place. What for example did it make you feel? When you have finished, stand back and look at all the places and together times. What do you feel when you see them all together like this?

Practical ways of enabling children to speak about feelings of loss

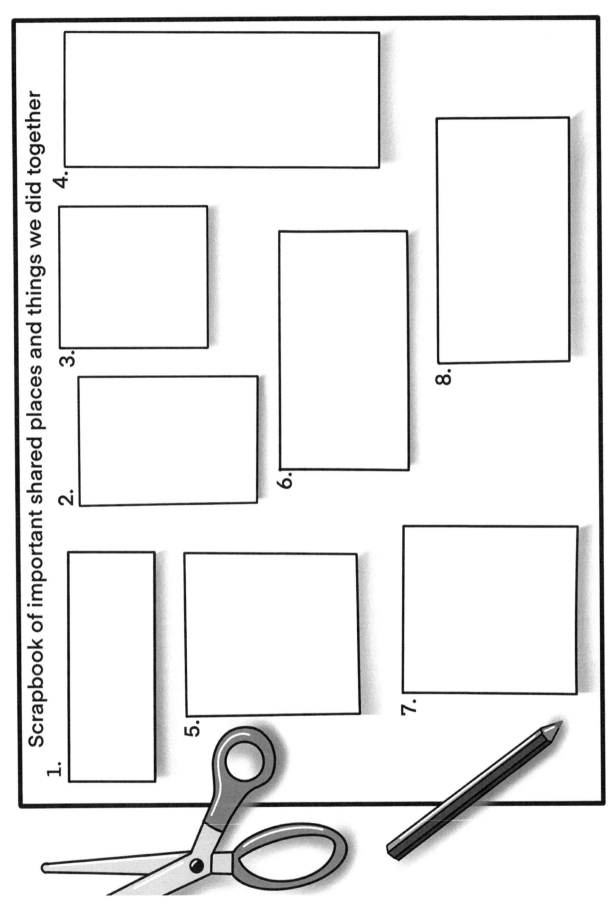

Scrapbook of important shared places and things we did together

Development

They might then want to write a little letter to the person they miss, telling them why the place or activity meant so much. You can offer to be the scribe. For example, *'Dear Dad, I loved playing football with you on a Sunday. You taught me so much about how to dribble and score and you looked so proud when I did it well. We had such fun didn't we Dad. I miss you so much.'* Then ask if they would like you to read it back to them.

Rejected/not wanted/left out

This exercise is relevant when you know a child has had a horrible experience of rejection, bullying, being left out etc. Experiences of rejection or being left out of a group or being told, 'We don't want you to play with us,' can trigger some of the worst pain we know. In fact, sometimes just one incident of rejection in childhood can lead to a social phobia, fear of meeting new people, or going to parties etc.

Research shows that feelings of rejection and underlying sense of social disconnection, trigger the same centres in the brain as those which trigger when we are in physical pain. (Eisenberger, 2012).

It is vital that these experiences are talked about and worked through with a listening other who can correct any negative self-beliefs. So this exercise gives a forum for that.

If you feel having done the exercise that the child is still locked in self-blame, support them to find appropriate empowered anger instead. If they are lost for words, you can speak to the rejectors. It's a technique called 'Speaking for the child.' Start by saying 'I might not get things right' so if after each sentence I speak, you think it's right, use the tinger (little bell or equivalent). If you think I've got it wrong, just stay silent.

Instructions to give to the child

Think of a time/times when you felt rejected, not wanted, uninvited. On the white slats on the door in the picture, write any words or feelings that come into your head. What did the horrible time make you feel about yourself? Did you manage to keep your self-esteem intact and realise that the rejection said far more about the rejecting person/people than you! If it still gets to you, would be prepared to speak now to the rejecters as if they were in the room? If so, great! It's easy. Just 'finish the sentence':

What I feel about you is . . .
I feel angry because . . .
I feel sad because . . .
I feel hurt because . . . .
If something similar happens again I'll . . .

Practical ways of enabling children to speak about feelings of loss

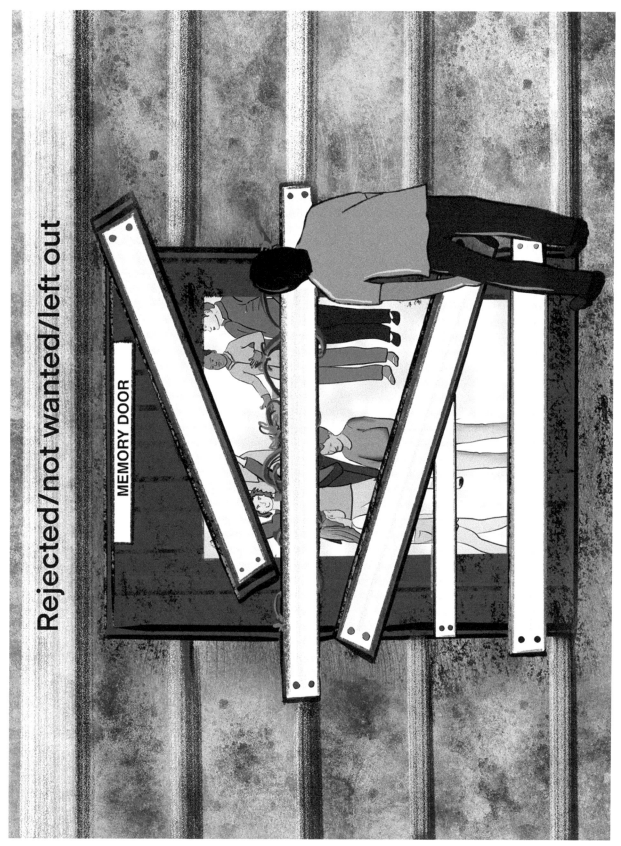

Development

Work with the child on words they can say if next time someone is mean to them or excluding.

Give them the psychoeducation that people are only mean if someone has been mean to them. Some parents don't know that children need to be treated with just as much respect as grown-ups. But when children have been treated cruelly or meanly they often try to make other children feel as they have been made to feel. So there's no point taking it personally. You have just become part of their story for that time.

On the outside of the group

Objective

Being in groups is often such an emotive subject, and too many of us never tell someone about those key memories of active rejection from a group: being left out, not wanted, uninvited. Yet these events always need processing/reflecting on with someone who is really good at listening to and finding words for our pain. Remember that suppressing feelings is really bad for mental and physical health. One study found that suppression of feelings increased the risk of cancer by 70 per cent (Chapman et al., 2013). So the objective of this exercise is to help the child to tell you the story of painful events that fall into this category. For some children, it might be feeling on the outside of a group after moving into a new house with stepchildren, resulting from a parent's new partnering. For other children the active exclusion might be due to some awful discrimination, due to the colour of their skin, religious differences, differences of culture, differences in sexual choices. For some children, it might be their own parent who can't accept their different choices, e.g. in religion, in lifestyle in sexual or gender preferences. For some children, depending on their actual experience of active exclusion, it may really help to talk about intolerance of difference in the world, and if the child is old enough, to give some historical context. This can help a child to appreciate the wider social context and how sadly many people are not able to celebrate difference and so remain intolerant of it. That said, there is far more awareness of the terrible social injustice of intolerance of difference globally and certainly a real change in some areas of the world, e.g. Western world over acceptance of difference of sexual choices. Of course, this context-giving would not be relevant to young children unless couched in simple language but for older children it can be bring a rich discourse and help the child to take less personally the social injustice they have suffered.

Instructions to give to the child

Look at the drawing and think of a time/times when you felt outside of a group now or in the past. For example, other children have used this drawing to describe an experience of being bullied at school, or not feeling accepted by a group of children who are already friends, and you are the new girl or boy. Others have used it to talk about horrible experiences of not being accepted due to being different in some way to the group.

Think what you felt at the time and what you felt about yourself? Write that in the memory circle or, if you like, write something else in the memory circle that was important about the event and what you learnt from it.

Practical ways of enabling children to speak about feelings of loss

On the outside of the group

Memories

Development

If what the child is taking away from the experience is somehow self-denigrating, e.g. *'I learnt that I am not good enough.' 'I learnt that I will never be one of the popular girls,'* voice other realities, e.g. that the group was insensitive or outright rejecting rather than the situation being about their failings.

Some children may also appreciate talking more generally about groups and their effect, by thinking of films, books, plays, actual historical events, particularly those which have some resonance with their own experience of groups. I have found some children to draw useful analogies for their own experiences of groups with those depicted in William Golding's *Lord of the Flies* for example.

With older children or teenagers you might also like to discuss the psychology of groups: how, for example, many groups need to have a scapegoat or an opposing group as an enemy or target to give them a purpose and make them feel more united.

No one listens/too unhelped

Objective
(More appropriate for older children, aged 9–13)

This exercise is suitable for older children who can understand, when explained to them, what misconnection and failed connection are, and the importance of repairing relationships that are worthy of repair.

The exercise focuses on times when you feel utterly alone because someone important didn't listen, understand, or help when they could have helped. Such painful events can leave a lasting impression and particularly in contexts such as a breach of trust, a betrayal, an awful disappointment or let down, or a realisation that the other person is incapable at this time of understanding something you desperately needed them to understand.

In relationship to family members or friends that really matter, these attachment ruptures can happen at a time of real need. This means the aloneness is even more painful. Furthermore, from such failed connections, a child/young person may form negative core beliefs about themselves and others such as *'I'm not worth listening to,' 'I can never get people to understand me,' 'My needs are unimportant.'*

This exercise is therefore designed to focus on unforgettable moments of failed connection, so that they can be reflected on, grieved, acknowledged by the listening other, and worked through. Then if appropriate and possible, resolved with the other person.

Instructions to give to the child
Times of misconnection and failed connection with people who were or are hugely important to us form vital aspects of our life story. We never forget them. It is important that these times are not just pushed away into our memory store where they can turn into bitterness or cold resentment, but rather shared with someone you trust so that they can be fully made sense of and worked through.

So think of a memory or memories of painful times in your life when you felt very alone because of a failed connection with another person. That person did not try to understand what you were feeling. They did not ask you what you were feeling, and they could have helped but they didn't help.

Practical ways of enabling children to speak about feelings of loss

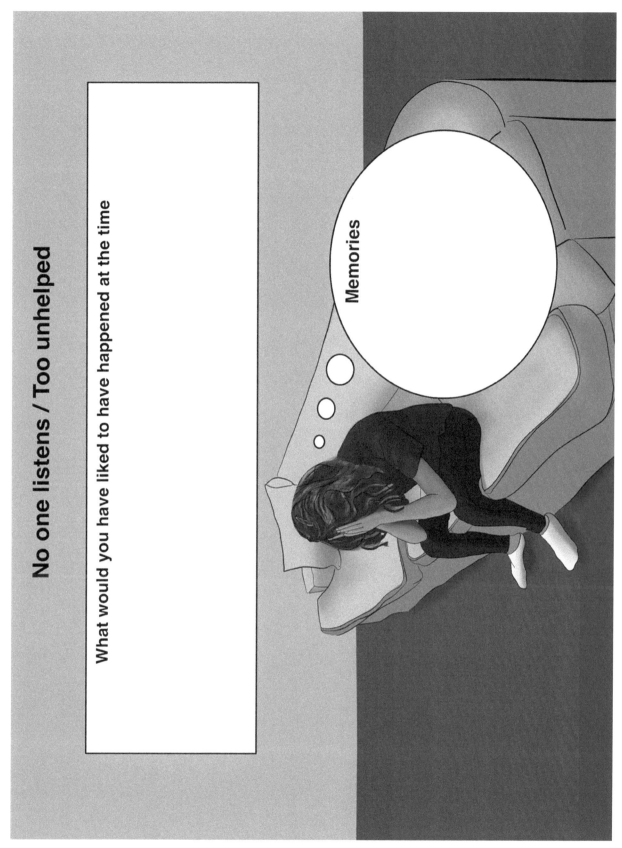

No one listens / Too unhelped

What would you have liked to have happened at the time

Memories

Now look at the picture. In the 'Memories circle,' write a title for each of the memories Then write in the box provided, what you would have liked to have happened at the time but it didn't.

Development

You might also want to ask children about the opposite, namely moments of real connection that again they will never forget. These need to be heard just as much as those misconnections. To enrich the dialogue, you might like to ask the child to think of books, plays or films they know where there have been memorable moments of connection and memorable moments of misconnection and how these have resonated with their own experiences.

The end of the relationship: what now?

Objective
(More appropriate for children over the age of 10.)

When a key relationship in your life ends, or is about to end, or is ending in the way you have known it previously, for many people it feels like a part of them has died, a part of their life has ended, and/or life has lost meaning. Due to the sheer pain of the feelings of loss it can be difficult to think well, because feelings are flooding the thinking part of your brain. So, this exercise is to support the child to let both their irrational voice and rational voice have a say. When worst fantasies are written down (rather than left swirling around in your mind as awful ruminations) they can be checked against reality, particularly when in the presence of a thinking compassionate other.

This exercise is particularly suitable for children and young people experiencing the rejection of a best friend or boyfriend or girlfriend, or a different severing say with death or a parent who walks away and doesn't return, or returns so occasionally it feels like the end of the relationship (such as after a parental separation/divorce).

Instructions to give to the child
Now that this important relationship in your life has ended or is about to end or end in the way that you have known it, and you are feeling the pain of that, it's really good to stand back and ask, 'What next?' On the picture, write down your worst fear and fantasies about what might happen next. Allow yourself to be as extreme as you like. Don't censor your fears. Then in the 'coping strategies' circle write down what you have not lost, namely your resources, your strengths, your friendships, your hobbies, your courage in seeking comfort. This circle may also include some lovely memories about the relationship that has ended if you want to include them.

When you have done this, stand back. Imagine the 'worst fantasies' were written by a far younger child part of you. Talk to her or him. What would you say to reassure her or him? How are other painful events in your life colouring and increasing the pain you are feeling now? Now talk on whatever level you feel comfortable about what is in the coping strategies circle.

What do you particularly value in terms of what you have written there?

Practical ways of enabling children to speak about feelings of loss

The end of the relationship: what now?

Worst fantasies

Coping strategies

Development

Writing a poem or doing a drawing about the loss can be hugely therapeutic. The act of symbolising in this way, as we saw in Chapter 2, is about taking back power so, as Angus and Greenberg (2011) says, 'You are having the emotion rather than the emotion having you!'

If age appropriate, offer the following quotations to the child. Discuss which quotations the child can relate to and why.

Her absence is like the sky, spread over everything. (C.S. Lewis, 1966)

Comforter, where, where is your comforting?' (Gerard Manley Hopkins, 1970)

Water, water everywhere nor any drop to drink. (Coleridge, 1992)

I'd walk down and I'd stare at the house for ages ... I'd keep saying it in my head – "He's dead, he's dead, he's dead." But it didn't mean anything. (Rosemary Dinnage, 1990)

What helps in breaking up is a reminder that there isn't much to do except to grieve and hurt. (Susie Orbach, 1994)

First Aid Box

Objective
This exercise is to remind the child of all the good things they still have in their life despite the awful loss.

If the child has a full and impressive First Aid Box, really affirm how smart they are to be able to remind him or herself of all the richness in his life at a time like this. If the child is 'avoidant attached,' with an expressed view of 'when the going gets tough the only person I can trust is myself,' it might be appropriate to talk of how people take that attitude to life when too many people have let them down in some way or been intrusive or abandoning. Older children often value the concept of 'blocked trust' (Hughes et al., 2019) and find it useful. Remember it's never too late to move to a life-attitude of trust and it may well happen with you.

Instructions to give to the child
When life gets tough or you've had an awful shock, it can feel like everything is smashed up. So it's important to remind yourself of the good things in your life that are *not* smashed up. These can include activities you enjoy, people in your life who really matter to you and with whom you feel very seen, valued and nourished. Write these on the first aid box. You can also include qualities you like about yourself, particularly during hard times like this.

If you find it difficult to think of good healing things to write in your box to nurture yourself at these difficult times, think whether perhaps you have a critical voice in your head rather than a compassionate one. It is never too late to change the former to the latter particularly with when spending time with a practitioner who is helping you think about your life and your feelings.

Practical ways of enabling children to speak about feelings of loss

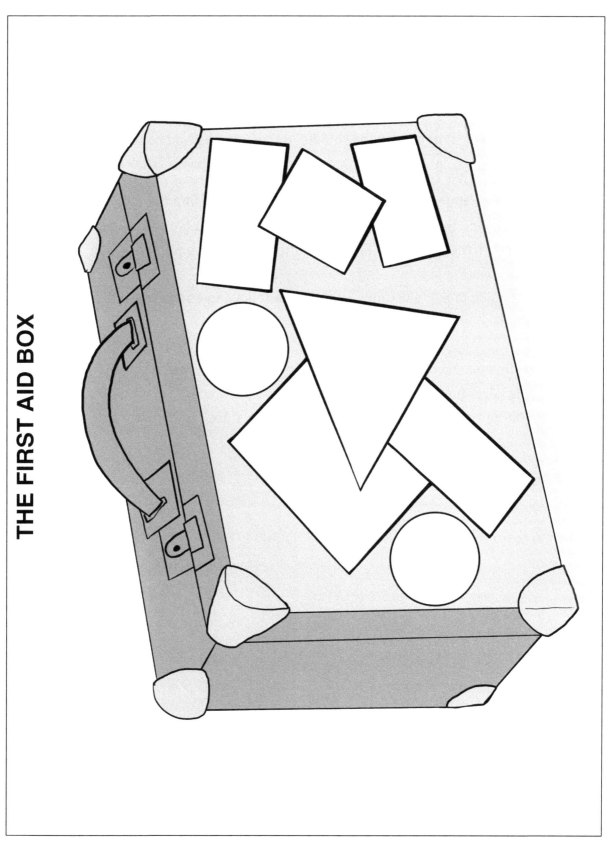

THE FIRST AID BOX

Development

This exercise involves sandplay. You will need a sandbox with a large selection of miniatures and objects. See the book *Using Storytelling as a Therapeutic Tool for Children* (Sunderland, 2001), if you need more information on how to use sandplay.

You may prefer to do a 'line down the middle' using crayons and paper instead.

Instructions to give to the child

Draw a line in the sand right down the middle of the box. Using the miniature objects and figures, show on the left-hand side in the sandbox what life was like before you lost this person and on the right what life is like after you lost the person.

You might then like to ask questions such as the following as appropriate for this particular child:

What do you feel when you look at the before and after pictures?
Are there any silver linings or is it too early to say?
Is there anything you want to change in either of the sides? (e.g. remove or add a figure)

Bibliography

2013. *Diagnostic and statistical manual of mental disorders*. Washington, DC, American Psychiatric Publishing.

2017. *Diagnostic and statistical manual of mental disorders*. Arlington, VA, American Psychiatric Association.

2021. *Sense of belonging scale*. [online] Imperial College London. Available at: www.imperial.ac.uk/education-research/evaluation/what-can-i-evaluate/sense-of-belonging/tools-for-assessing-sense-of-belonging/sense-of-belonging-scale/ (Accessed 12 July 2021)

Alvarez, A., 1971. *The Savage God: A Study of Suicide*. Harmondsworth, Penguin.

American Psychiatric Association, 1994, *Diagnostic and Statistical Manual of Mental Disorders: DSM-IV* 4th edn, Washington, DC, American Psychiatric Association.

Anda, R., Williamson, D., Macera, C., Eaker, E., Glassman, A., Marks, J., 1993, Depressed affect, hopelessness, and the risk of ischemic heart disease in a cohort of U.S. adults. *Epidemiology*, 4(4), 285–294.

Angus, L. and Greenberg, L., 2011. *Working With Narrative in Emotion-Focused Therapy*. Washington, DC, American Psychological Association.

Arslan, G., 2018. Understanding the association between school belonging and emotional health in adolescents. *International Journal of Educational Psychology*, 7(1), 21.

Bakwin, H., 1941. Loneliness in infants. *Archives of Pediatrics & Adolescent Medicine*, 63(1), 30.

Barriguete-Meléndez, J., Pérez-Bustinzar, A., de la Vega-Morales, R., Córdova-Villalobos, J., Sánchez-González, J., Barriguete-Chávez Peón, P. and Rojo-Moreno, L., 2019. Prevalence of alexithymia in eating disorders in a clinical sample of 800 Mexican patients. *Cirugía y Cirujanos (English Edition)*, 86(1).

Bateman, A. and Fonagy, P., 2010. Mentalization based treatment for borderline personality disorder. *World Psychiatry*, 9(1), 11–15.

BBC, 2021. *Joey Essex: Grief and Me*. [video] Available at: www.bbc.co.uk/programmes/p09hy0vh (Accessed 11 June 2021).

Berthelot, N., Lemieux, R., Garon-Bissonnette, J., Lacharité, C. and Muzik, M., 2019. The protective role of mentalizing: Reflective functioning as a mediator between child maltreatment, psychopathology and parental attitude in expecting parents. *Child Abuse & Neglect*, 95.

Bollas, C. (1987). *The Shadow of the Object: Psychoanalysis of the Unthought Known*. London, Free Association Books.

Bibliography

Borelli, J, Cohen, C., Pettit, C., Normandin, L., Target, M., Fonagy P., Ensink, 2019. Maternal and child sexual abuse history: An intergenerational exploration of children's adjustment and maternal trauma-reflective functioning. May 14. *Frontiers in Psychology*, 10, 1062.

Bowlby, J., 1973. *Attachment and Loss: Volume 2 – Separation, Anxiety and Anger*. London, Hogarth Press.

Bowlby, J., 1978. *Attachment and Loss: Volume 3 – Loss, Sadness and Depression*. Harmondsworth, Penguin.

Bowlby, J., 1979. *The Making and Breaking of Affectional Bonds*. London, Tavistock.

Bowlby, 1981, Psychoanalysis as a natural science. Delivered as the 1980 University College London Freud Memorial Lecture and published in Volume 8 of *International Review of Psychoanalysis*, 1980.

Bowlby, J., 1988. *A Secure Base: Clinical Applications of Attachment Theory*. London, Routledge.

Bowlby, J., 1999. *Attachment and Loss*. New York, Basic Books.

Buber M., 1987, *I and Thou* (Gregor Smith R. trans.), Edinburgh, T & T Clark. (First published 1937.)

Burkhart, M., Borelli, J., Rasmussen, H., Brody, R. and Sbarra, D., 2017. Parental mentalizing as an indirect link between attachment anxiety and parenting satisfaction. *Journal of Family Psychology*, 31(2), 203–213.

Burklund, L., Creswell, J., Irwin, M. and Lieberman, M., 2014. The common and distinct neural bases of affect labeling and reappraisal in healthy adults. *Frontiers in Psychology*, 5.

Byatt, A.S., 1995. *Still Life*. New York/London, Vintage.

Cain, A., 2002. Children of suicide: The telling and the knowing. *Psychiatry: Interpersonal and Biological Processes*, 65(2), 124–136.

Camoirano, A., 2017. Mentalizing makes parenting work: a review about parental reflective functioning and clinical interventions to improve it. *Frontiers in Psychology*, 8.

Casagrande, M., Boncompagni, I., Forte, G., Guarino, A. and Favieri, F., 2019. Emotion and overeating behavior: Effects of alexithymia and emotional regulation on overweight and obesity. *Eating and Weight Disorders – Studies on Anorexia, Bulimia and Obesity*, 25(5), 1333–1345.

Casement, P., 2013. *On Learning From the Patient*. London, Routledge.

Cerutti, R., Spensieri, V., Valastro, C., Presaghi, F., Canitano, R. and Guidetti, V., 2017. A comprehensive approach to understand somatic symptoms and their impact on emotional and psychosocial functioning in children. *PLOS ONE*, 12(2).

Chapman, B., Fiscella, K., Kawachi, I., Duberstein, P. and Muennig, P., 2013. Emotion suppression and mortality risk over a 12-year follow-up. *Journal of Psychosomatic Research*, 75(4), 381–385.

Chester, D., Eisenberger, N., Pond, R., Richman, S., Bushman, B., DeWall, C., 2013. The interactive effect of social pain and executive functioning on aggression: An fMRI experiment. *Social Cognitive and Affective Neuroscience*, 2013, 1–6.

Clanchy, K., n.d. *Some kids I taught and what they taught me*. London, Picador.

Clarkson, P., 1989. *Gestalt Counselling in Action*. London, Sage.

Coleman, J., 1999, *Key Data on Adolescence*, London, Trust for the Study of Adolescence.

Coleridge, S.T., The Rime of the Ancient Mariner, in *Selected Poetry* (Penguin Classics) Paperback – 17 April 2000.

de Botton, A., 2020. *Anxiety: Meditations on the Anxious Mind*. London, The School of Life Press.

De Roo, M., Wong, G., Rempel, G. and Fraser, S., 2019. Advancing optimal development in children: Examining the construct validity of a parent reflective functioning questionnaire. *JMIR Pediatrics and Parenting*, 2(1).

de Roos, C., Greenwald, R., den Hollander-Gijsman, M., Noorthoorn, E., van Buuren, S. and de Jongh, A., 2011. A randomised comparison of cognitive behavioural therapy (CBT) and eye movement desensitisation and reprocessing (EMDR) in disaster-exposed children. *European Journal of Psychotraumatology*, 2(1).

Dillon, A., Timulak, L., and Greenberg, L.S., 2016. Transforming core emotional pain in a course of emotion-focused therapy for depression: A case study. *Psychotherapy Research*, 11, 1–17.

Dinnage R., 1990, *The Ruffian on the Stair: Reflections on Death*. London, Viking.

Eerdewegh, M.M. van, Clayton, P.J. & Eerdewegh P. van, 1985, The bereaved child: Variables influencing early psychopathology, *British Journal of Psychiatry*, 147, 188–194.

Eisenberger, N., 2003. Does rejection hurt? An fMRI study of social exclusion. *Science*, 302(5643), 290–292.

Eisenberger, N., 2012. The pain of social disconnection: Examining the shared neural underpinnings of physical and social pain. *Nature Reviews Neuroscience*, May 3, 13(6), 421–434.

Eisenberger, N., 2012. The pain of social disconnection: Examining the shared neural underpinnings of physical and social pain. *Nature Reviews Neuroscience*, 13(6), 421–434.

Eliot, T.S., 1990, *Collected Poems 1909–1962*. London, Faber & Faber. (Original work published 1936 as Collected Poems.)

Evans, C. & Millard, A., 1995, *Greek Myths and Legends*. London, Usborne.

Fang, S., Chung, M. and Wang, Y., 2020. The impact of past trauma on psychological distress: The roles of defense mechanisms and alexithymia. *Frontiers in Psychology*, 11.

Felitti, V., 2019. Health appraisal and the adverse childhood experiences study: National implications for health care, cost, and utilization. *The Permanente Journal*, 23, 18–26.

Fisher, L., Overholser, J., Ridley, J., Braden, A. and Rosoff, C., 2015. From the outside looking in: Sense of belonging, depression, and suicide risk. *Psychiatry*, 78(1), 29–41.

Fonagy, P. and Bateman, A., 2006. Mechanisms of change in mentalization-based treatment of BPD. *Journal of Clinical Psychology*, 62(4), 411–430.

Fonagy, P. and Bateman, A., 2009. Randomized controlled trial of outpatient mentalization-based treatment versus structured clinical management for borderline personality disorder. *American Journal of Psychiatry*, 166 (12), 1355–1364.

Fonagy, P., Gergely, G., Jurist, E., Target, M., 2002. *Affect Regulation, Mentalization, and the Development of the Self*. New York, Other Press.

Fonagy, P., Steele, M., Steele, H., Moran, G. and Higgitt, A., 1991. The capacity for understanding mental states: the reflective self in parent and child and its significance for security of attachment. *Infant Mental Health Journal*, 12(3), 201–218.

Fonagy, P. and Target, M., 1998. Mentalization and the changing aims of child psychoanalysis. *Psychoanalytic Dialogues*, 8(1), 87–114.

Freud, S., 1909. *Selected papers on hysteria and other psychoneuroses*. 4th ed. New York, The Journal of Nervous and Mental Disease Publishing Company.

Freud, S., 1915. 'Repression', in *Sigmund Freud: The Collected Works of Sigmund Freud*. Pergamon Press.

Freud, S., 1917. General Theory of the Neuroses (1916–17) In *Introductory Lectures on Psycho-Analysis (Part 3)*, in Strachey, J. London, Vintage. (2001).

Freud S., 1979. 'Inhibitions, Symptoms and Anxiety', in *On Psychopathology, Inhibitions, Symptoms and Anxiety*, Vol. 10 of The Penguin Freud Library, Richards A. and Strachey J. (eds), Strachey J. (trans), Harmondsworth, Penguin. pp. 237–333. (First published 1926.)

Freud S., 1984. 'Mourning and Melancholia', in *On Metapsychology: The Theory of Psychoanalysis*, Vol 11 of The Pelican Freud Library, London, Penguin. pp. 245–268. (First published 1917.)

Freud S., 1991. 'General Theory of the Neuroses', in *Introductory Lectures on Psychoanalysis*, Vol. 1 of The Penguin Freud Library, Richards A. and Strachey J. (eds), Strachey J. (trans), Harmondsworth, Penguin. pp. 281–517. (First published 1917.)

Fristad M.A., Jedel R., Weller R.A. and Weller E.B., 1993. Psychosocial functioning in children after the death of a parent. *American Journal of Psychiatry*, 150(3), 511–513.

Geddes, H., 2006. *Attachment in the Classroom*. London, Worth Publishing.

Goodall J., 1990. *Through a Window: Thirty Years with the Chimpanzees of Gombe*. London, Weidenfeld & Nicolson.

Gottman, J.M., Katz, L.F., and Hooven, C., 1996. Parental meta-emotion philosophy and the emotional life of families: Theoretical models and preliminary data. *Journal of Family Psychology*, 10(3), 243–268.

Gracanin, A., Bylsma, L. and Vingerhoets, A., 2014. Is crying a self-soothing behavior? *Frontiers in Psychology*, 5.

Hagerty, B., Lynch-Sauer, J., Patusky, K., Bouwsema, M. and Collier, P., 1992. Sense of belonging: A vital mental health concept. *Archives of Psychiatric Nursing*, 6(3), 172–177.

Hagerty, B., Williams, R., Coyne, J. and Early, M., 1996. Sense of belonging and indicators of social and psychological functioning. *Archives of Psychiatric Nursing*, 10(4), 235–244.

Harlow H.F. and Mears C., 1979, *Primate Perspectives*, New York/London, John Wiley.

Harper, D. and Moss, D., 2003. A different kind of chemistry? Reformulating 'formulation'. *Clinical Psychology*, 25, 6–10.

Harris-Hendriks J., 1993, *When Father Kills Mother: Guiding Children Through Trauma and Grief*. London, Routledge.

Harvard Graduate School of Education, 2020. Making Caring Common Project. *Listening Deeply Strategy* [podcast]. Available at: https://mcc.gse.harvard.edu/resources-for-educators/listening-deeply-strategy. (Accessed 27 May 2021).

Heinicke C. and Westheimer I., 1966. *Brief Separations*. New York, International Universities Press.

Herman N., 1987. *Why Psychotherapy?* London, Free Association Books.

Herman, J., 1998. Recovery from psychological trauma. *Psychiatry and Clinical Neurosciences*, 52(S1).

Herman, J., 2015. *The Aftermath of Violence – From Domestic Abuse to Political Terror*. 7 July 2015, London, Basic Books.

Holmes, S., Johnson, N. and Johnson, D., 2019. Understanding the relationship between interpersonal trauma and disordered eating: An extension of the model of psychological adaptation. *Psychological Trauma: Theory, Research, Practice, and Policy*.

Holt-Lunstad, J., Smith, T., Baker, M., Harris, T. and Stephenson, D., 2015. Loneliness and social isolation as risk factors for mortality. *Perspectives on Psychological Science*, 10(2), pp. 227–237.

Honkalampi, K., Hintikka, J., Tanskanen, A., Lehtonen, J. and Viinamäki, H., 2000. Depression is strongly associated with alexithymia in the general population. *Journal of Psychosomatic Research*, 48(1), 99–104.

Hopkins, G.M., 1985. *Poems and Prose*. Gardner W.H. (ed.), Penguin. (First published 1918.)

Hughes, D., 2018. *Personal communication with Dr Dan Hughes*.

Hughes, D., Golding, K. and Hudson, J., 2019. *Healing Relational Trauma with Attachment-Focused Interventions*. New York, W.W. Norton & Co.

Jeffers, S.J., 2012. *Feel the Fear and Do it Anyway*. Vermilion, Special Edition, 5 April 2012.

Johnstone, L. and Boyle, M., 2018. *The Power Threat Meaning Framework*. The British Psychological Society.

Karukivi, M., Hautala, L., Kaleva, O., Haapasalo-Pesu, K., Liuksila, P., Joukamaa, M. and Saarijärvi, S., 2010. Alexithymia is associated with anxiety among adolescents. *Journal of Affective Disorders*, 125(1–3), 383–387.

Kehinde, F., Bharmal, A., Goodyer, I., Kelvin, R., Dubicka, B., Midgley, N., Fonagy, P., Jones, P. and Wilkinson, P., 2021. Cross-sectional and longitudinal associations between psychotic and depressive symptoms in depressed adolescents. *European Child & Adolescent Psychiatry*.

Khan, A., Dar, S., Ahmed, R., Bachu, R., Adnan, M. and Kotapati, V., 2018. Cognitive behavioral therapy versus eye movement desensitization and reprocessing in patients with post-traumatic stress disorder: Systematic review and meta-analysis of randomized clinical trials. *Cureus*.

Kiema, H., Rantanen, A., Laukka, S., Siipo, A. and Soini, H., 2014. The connection between skilled counseling and client's heart rate variability. *Procedia - Social and Behavioral Sciences*, 159, 802–807.

Kircanski, K., Lieberman, M. and Craske, M., 2012. Feelings into words. *Psychological Science*, 23(10), 1086–1091.

Klein, M., 1997. *Envy and Gratitude and Other Works 1946–1963*. Penguin Vintage Classics, Reprint edition (6 November 1997).

Kotulak R., 1997. *Inside the Brain: Revolutionary Discoveries of How the Mind Works*. Kansas City, Andrews McMeel Publishing.

Lane, R., Ryan, L., Nadel, L. and Greenberg, L. (2015). Memory reconsolidation, emotional arousal, and the process of change in psychotherapy: New insights from brain science, *Behavioral and Brain Sciences*, 38.

Levi P., 1986, *Moments of Reprieve*, Feldman R. (trans), London, Abacus.

Lewis C.S., 1966, *A Grief Observed*, London, Faber & Faber. (First published 1961.)

Lumley, M., Asselin, L. and Norman, S., 1997. Alexithymia in chronic pain patients. *Comprehensive Psychiatry*, 38(3), 160–165.

Lyvers, M., Brown, T. and Thorberg, F., 2018. Is it the taste or the buzz? Alexithymia, caffeine, and emotional eating. *Substance Use & Misuse*, 54(4), 572–582.

Malda-Castillo, J., Browne, C. and Perez-Algorta, G., 2018. Mentalization-based treatment and its evidence-base status: A systematic literature review. *Psychology and Psychotherapy: Theory, Research and Practice*, 92(4), 465–498.

Maslow, A., 1943. A theory of human motivation. *Psychological Review*, 50(4), 370–396.

Masters, B., 1985, *Killing for Company: The Case of Dennis Nilsen*. London, Cape.

Maté, G., 2019. What the REAL cause of your anxiety is – With Dr Gabor Maté, *Human Window*. www.youtube.com/watch?v=39RyGEVRbWk.

McDougall J., 1989, *Theatres of the Body: Psychoanalytic Approach to Psychosomatic Illness*. London, Free Association Books.

Mental Health Foundation, 1999. *The Fundamental Facts: All the Latest Facts and Figures on Mental Illness*, London, Mental Health Foundation.

Mental Health Foundation, October 2018, The Make It Count Campaign, London www.mentalhealth.org.uk/sites/default/files/make-it-count-policy-briefing.pdf.

Mitchell S., 1988, *Relational Concepts in Psychoanalysis: An Integration*. New York, Guildford.

Montagu A., 1971, *Touching: The Human Significance of the Skin*. London, Harper & Row.

Moore T., 1992. *Care of the Soul: A Guide for Cultivating Depth and Sacredness in Everyday Life*. New York, HarperCollins.

Morelli, S., Torre, J. and Eisenberger, N., 2014. The neural bases of feeling understood and not understood. *Social Cognitive and Affective Neuroscience*, 9(12), 1890–1896.

Murray L., 1997. *Subhuman Redneck Poems*. Manchester, Carcanet.

Neulinger, S., 2021. The Treatment of Sexual Abuse. *Conference Centre for Child Mental Health*. June 2021.

Nhlbi.nih.gov. 2021. *Heart disease and depression: A two-way relationship | NHLBI, NIH*. [online] Available at: www.nhlbi.nih.gov/news/2017/heart-disease-and-depression-two-way-relationship. (Accessed 11 June 2021).

O'Keeffe, P., 2021. *A sense of belonging: Improving student retention*. [online] Available at: www.researchgate.net/publication/319523471_A_sense_of_belonging_Improving_student_retention (Accessed 12 July 2013).

Orbach S., 1994, *What's Really Going On Here?* London, Virago.

Ovid, 1995, *Orpheus in the Underworld*, Innes M. (trans), Harmondsworth, Penguin.

Panksepp, J., 1998. *Affective Neuroscience: The Foundations of Human and Animal Emotions*. Oxford, Oxford University Press.

Panksepp, J., 2021. *From psychiatric ward to happiness*. [image] Available at: www.youtube.com/watch?v=Xevjwe1qQ7c (Accessed 11 June 2021).

Panksepp, J. and Biven, L., 2012. *The Archaeology of Mind: Neuroevolutionary Origins of Human Emotion*. New York, W.W. Norton.

Panksepp, J. and Watt, D., 2011. Why does depression hurt? Ancestral primary-process separation-distress (PANIC/GRIEF) and diminished brain reward (SEEKING) processes in the genesis of depressive affect. *Psychiatry: Interpersonal and Biological Processes*, 74(1), 5–13.

Patel, J., Berntson, J., Polanka, B. and Stewart, J., 2018. Cardiovascular risk factors as differential predictors of incident atypical and typical major depressive disorder in US adults. *Psychosomatic Medicine*, 80(6), 508–514.

Pellowski, A., 1977. *The World of Storytelling*. Bronx, NY, H.W. Wilson.

Pendergast, D., Allen, J., McGregor, G. and Ronksley-Pavia, M., 2018. Engaging marginalized, "at-risk" middle-level students: A focus on the importance of a sense of belonging at school. *Education Sciences*, 8(3), 138.

Plath S., 1981, *Collected Poems*. London, Faber & Faber.

Plato, 1951, *The Symposium*, Hamilton W. (trans), Harmondsworth, Penguin.

Bibliography

Klein, M., *Love, Guilt and Reparation and Other Works 1921–1945*, London, Virago. pp. 233–235.

Reid S., 1990, The importance of beauty in the psychoanalytic experience. *Journal of Child Psychotherapy*, 16(1), 29–52. (Originally given at a study weekend of the Association of Child Psychotherapy, March 1987.)

Rieffe, C. and De Rooij, M., 2012. The longitudinal relationship between emotion awareness and internalising symptoms during late childhood. *European Child & Adolescent Psychiatry*, 21(6), 349–356.

Rilke R.M., 1939, *The Duino Elegies*, Leishman J.B. and Spender S. (trans), New York, W.W. Norton.

Robertson J., 1953, *A Two-Year-Old Goes to Hospital*, Penn State Audio-Visual Services, University Park PA.

Robinson, P., Hellier, J., Barrett, B., Barzdaitiene, D., Bateman, A., Bogaardt, A., Clare, A., Somers, N., O'Callaghan, A., Goldsmith, K., Kern, N., Schmidt, U., Morando, S., Ouellet-Courtois, C., Roberts, A., Skårderud, F. and Fonagy, P., 2016. The nourished randomised controlled trial comparing mentalisation-based treatment for eating disorders (MBT-ED) with specialist supportive clinical management (SSCM-ED) for patients with eating disorders and symptoms of borderline personality disorder. *Trials*, 17(1).

Rossi, M., Bruno, G., Chiusalupi, M. and Ciaramella, A., 2018. Relationship between pain, somatisation, and emotional awareness in primary school children. *Pain Research and Treatment*, 2018, 1–12.

Rosso, A., Viterbori, P. and Scopesi, A., 2015. Are maternal reflective functioning and attachment security associated with preadolescent mentalization? *Frontiers in Psychology*, 6.

Schultheis, A., Mayes, L. and Rutherford, H., 2019. Associations between emotion regulation and parental reflective functioning. *Journal of Child and Family Studies*, 28(4), 1094–1104.

Scopesi, A., Rosso, A., Viterbori, P. and Panchieri, E., 2014. Mentalizing abilities in preadolescents' and their mothers' autobiographical narratives. *The Journal of Early Adolescence*, 35(4), 467–483.

Shipko, S., 1982. Alexithymia and somatization. *Psychotherapy and Psychosomatics*, 37(4), 193–201.

Speer, M., Bhanji, J. and Delgado, M., 2014. Savoring the past: Positive memories evoke value representations in the striatum. *Neuron*, 84(4), 847–856.

Speer, M. and Delgado, M., 2017. Reminiscing about positive memories buffers acute stress responses. *Nature Human Behaviour*, 1(5).

St-Amand, J., Girard, S. and Smith, J., 2017. Sense of belonging at school: Defining attributes, determinants, and sustaining strategies. *IAFOR Journal of Education*, 5(2).

Starr, L., Hershenberg, R., Shaw, Z., Li, Y. and Santee, A., 2020. The perils of murky emotions: Emotion differentiation moderates the prospective relationship between naturalistic stress exposure and adolescent depression. *Emotion*, 20(6), 927–938.

Stern D.N., 1993, 'Acting Versus Remembering in Transference Love and Infantile Love', in Spector Person E, Hagelin A. and Fonagy P. (eds), *On Freud's 'Observations on Transference-Love'*, New Haven/London, Yale University Press, pp. 172–185.

Strachey A. (ed), 1907, *The Letters of Edward Lear*, London, Fisher Unwin.

Sunderland M. and Armstrong N., 2003, *The Day the Sea Went Out and Never Came Back*, London, Routledge.

Sunderland M. and Armstrong N., 2018. *The Emotion Cards*. London, Routledge.

Sunderland M. & Armstrong N., 2018. *The Relationship Cards*. London, Routledge.

Sunderland M., 2001, *Using Storytelling as a Therapeutic Tool with Children*, Brackley, Speechmark Publishing.

Sylvers, P., Lilienfeld, S. and LaPrairie, J., 2011. Differences between trait fear and trait anxiety: Implications for psychopathology, *Clinical Psychology Review*, 31(1), 122–137.

The Conversation. 2021. *Can a lack of love be deadly?* [online] Available at: https://theconversation.com/can-a-lack-of-love-be-deadly-58659 (Accessed 11 June 2021).

The School of Life, 2019. *The one question we need to ask ourselves when we feel anxious.* [image] Available at: www.youtube.com/watch?v=D8Gc6_S6i0k (Accessed 16 June 2021).

Van der Kolk, B., 2015. *The Body Keeps the Score*. UK, Penguin Books.

Van der Kolk, D., 2021. *What is psychological trauma and what does it have to do with the body?* Conference, The Royal Society of Medicine, 24 June 2021.

Wilczyńska, A., Januszek, M. and Bargiel-Matusiewicz, K., 2015. The need of belonging and sense of belonging versus effectiveness of coping. *Polish Psychological Bulletin*, 46(1), 72–81.

Winnicott D.W., 1996, 'The Effect of Loss on The Young', Shepherd R., Johns J. & Robinson H.T. (eds), *D.W. Winnicott: Thinking About Children*. London, Karnac. (First published 1968.)

Wolpert L., 1999, *Malignant Sadness: The Anatomy of Depression*, London, Faber & Faber.

Woodman M., 1985, *The Pregnant Virgin: A Process of Psychological Transformation*, Toronto, CA, Inner City Books.

Yorke, M., 2014. The development and initial use of a survey of student 'belongingness', engagement and self-confidence in UK higher education. *Assessment & Evaluation in Higher Education*, 41(1), 154–166.

Index

acetylcholine 33, 35, 36
activities to enable speaking about loss: the end of the relationship 75–77; festival of moments 60–62; first aid box 78–80; life after losing a person or their love 57–59; museum of hurt 54–56; museum of loss 48–50; no one listens/too unhelped 72–74; on the outside of the group 69–71; rejected/not wanted/left out 66–68; scrapbook of important shared places and things 63–65; shock 45–47; when the pain of loss gets into everything 51–53
alexithymic 30
anger 33–36
Angus, L. 2, 38–39, 77
anxiety 37–42
artwork 13–14, 40–42
attachment 28, 30, 51
avoidant attachment 30, 78

Biven, L. 35
bleakness 11–13
bottled up feelings 31–33
Bowlby, J. 18, 28, 29, 32, 51
brain chemicals 6–7, 33–34, 35–36

catastrophic fantasies 15
chimpanzee study 21
Clanchy, K. 41
corticotropin-releasing factor (CRF) 7, 34
crying 22, 32–33, 51

defending against pain 25–27
defensive anger 33–36

despair 20–24
discrimination 69
displacement 37

emotion cards 30
emotional needs 53
emotions: benefits of talking about 1; bottled up feelings 31–33, 57; cutting off the grief 27–30; defensive anger 33–36; despair/withdrawal and hopelessness 20–24; emptiness 11–14; fear 15–17; painful feelings 3, 6–11; shock 3–6; yearning, longing or searching 17–20
empathy 9, 34, 35, 48
empowerment 4–5, 40, 77
emptiness 11–14
end of the relationship 10, 75–77
exclusion, feeling of 69–71
expressing feelings 31–33
eye movement desensitisation and reprocessing (EMDR) 16–17

Fang, S. 1
fear 15–17, 37
festival of moments 60–62
first aid box 78–80
Freud, S. 32

Goodall, J. 21
goodbyes 10, 75–77
Greenberg, L. 2, 38–39, 77
grief: benefits of talking about 1–2; bottled up feelings 31–33, 57; crying 22, 32–33, 51; cutting off feelings 27–30; defensive anger 33–36; despair/withdrawal

and hopelessness 20–24; emptiness 11–14; fear 15–17; painful feelings 3, 6–11; shock 3–6; yearning, longing or searching 17–20
groups, exclusion from 69–71

health impacts of grief 1, 31
healthy anger 36
Herman, J. 40, 47
hopelessness 20–24
Hughes, D. 35

images to represent loss 1–2, 40–42

Jung, C. 40–41

Lane, R. 39
language: benefits of talking about loss 1–2; cutting off the grief 27; emotion cards 30; enabling children to speak about loss 43–44; love 22–23, 57–59; pain 7, 10–11; shock 4, 45; yearning, longing or searching 19; *see also* activities to enable speaking about loss
left out, sense of 66–71
Lewis, C. S. 8, 18, 24
loneliness 12, 20, 72–74
longing 17–20
love 6, 22–23, 57–59

Maté, G. 39
memories: festival of moments 60–62; not being listened to 72–74; reminiscing 19–20, 50, 60–62; scrapbook of important shared places and things 63–65
mental states 1
Murray, L. 37
museum of hurt 54–56

Neulinger, S. B. 35
neurochemistry 6–7, 33–34, 35–36

obsessive compulsive disorder (OCD) 37
opioids in the brain 7, 33, 35
oxytocin 6, 35

pain of loss: images and metaphors 21–22; strength of 3, 6–11; when the pain of loss gets into everything 51–53
painful feelings: cutting off the grief 27–30; defending against 25–27; leading to anxiety 37–42; *see also* emotions
panic attacks 37
Panksepp, J. 6–7, 35
parental separation 18, 28
photos 20, 62
platitudes 21–22
poetry 41, 77
post-traumatic stress disorder (PTSD) 6, 16–17
power 4–5, 40, 77
psychoeducation 4
psychological safety 40
puberty 38

reassurances 9–10
Redford, A. 30
rejection 66–71
relationship cards 30
reminiscing 19–20, 50, 60–62

safety, psychological 40
sandplay 14, 23–24, 56, 80
scrapbook of important shared places and things 63–65
searching 17–20
self-blame 66

Index

serotonin 34
Shakespeare, W. 30, 31
shock 3–6, 32, 38, 45–47
story telling 38–39, 40, 69
story writing 13

teenage years 38
timing 9, 22
traumatic loss for children 1–3, 25–26, 33–34, 37–38
trust 78

underregulated emotion 1–2

Van der Kolk, B. 40

withdrawal 20–24
words: benefits of talking about loss 1–2; cutting off the grief 27; emotion cards 30; enabling children to speak about loss 43–44; love 22–23, 57–59; pain 7, 10–11; shock 4, 45; yearning, longing or searching 19; *see also* activities to enable speaking about loss

yearning 17–20